# Coffee Poems

# Coffee Poems

*reflections on life with coffee*

Edited by
## Lorraine Healy

World Enough
Writers

Poetry
ISBN 978-1-937797-08-9

Cover photo by Lorraine Healy

Lorraine Healy photo by Dianne MoonDancer

Book Text and Cover Design by Tonya Namura using Adobe Jenson Pro

World Enough Writers
PO Box 445
Tillamook. OR 97141

http://WorldEnoughWriters.com

WorldEnoughWriters@gmail.com

*Without coffee, nothing gets written. Period.*

—Nancy Kress

# INTRODUCTION

What struck me most as I read the submissions for this anthology was the sheer amount of new vocabulary which accompanied that old plain staple of the café or the diner, the cup of coffee. Cell phones and their cameras, roasters, vegan cake, baristas, soy lattes, drive-through windows, macchiato, McDonald's, Apple Pay. Maxwell and Folgers turned into Starbucks ubiquity, coffee-pots that wake before us and offer that first hot hit of the day. As a child moved from the bottle to milky café con leche, as a native of a city so imbued by coffee that index and thumb two inches apart signals espresso, it made me wonder about this new age of *coffea arabica*.

"The fashion in Berkeley, it's just like New York" observes Alicia Ostriker in "Berkeley: Youth and Age." As it is in Marseille, Venice, Limassol, Barcelona. But the secret ceremonies of milk and sugar, early morning, and the blue-collared world are here as well. Whether central to the poem or sitting on a side table, a mere accessory; whether a prop in an internal conversation with a *you* absent these 25 years or a desperately needed substance without which there is no facing the day, a cup of coffee inhabits each of these poems. "Coffee is my mother now" writes Laura Cherry in her poem "The Knot." There are so many ways to be orphaned...

Breathe in the scent and may it keep you awake.

Lorraine Healy, editor
2019

# TABLE OF CONTENTS

## i. At the Cafe

## ii. Home Grounds

## iii. Literary Latte

## iv. Elegy with Coffee

## v. The Coffee Between Us

# Coffee
# Poems

*reflections on life with coffee*

# i.

# At the Café

*These coffee shops and bookshops, these cafés and bars,*
*their sole owner is you.*

—Kamand Kojouri

# A DECEMBER SUNRISE

In the dark each minute anticipates
one more step into a brighter sky.
Colors with red thoughts gather
in the eastern horizon. Soon,
they cover the whole sky.

The first sunlight of the day,
like a newborn's hand,
touches the poem's face.
A compass points to a cloud
and all the metaphors orient.

Some words insist on taking the poem
up into the sky. These words are
larger than their bodies and they make
oceanic waves in a few syllables.
They overwhelm the other words.

The poem decides to leave them outside
and enters the coffeehouse.
Soon, the warm air and the coffee smell
settle
on the notebook.

## CAFFÈ CORRETTO AL VINAVIL

Invidio l'ordine
dei bicchieri tutti in fila
e la schiera di bottiglie colorate
al bar—la mattina
nei clacson da girare
insieme allo zucchero.
È complicato restare
guardando fisso dentro la tazza
senza annegare il grigio abitudine
tra il cielo e la terra
immobile—come il bianco
nei miei occhi quando cieco
e scivolo.
Cerco un attacco soltanto
sul silenzio d'acciaio
dei miei sorsi vuoti
poi mi rimetto l'anima in borsa
e vado.

Francesca Pellegrino
Adria Bernardi (translator)

# CAFFÈ CORRETTO WITH VINAVIL

I envy the order of glasses
in a line
and colored bottles in a row
at the bar in the morning
the honking getting stirred in
with sugar.
It's difficult to stand
staring into the cup
without drowning the gray mundane
between sky and concrete
earth so like the whites
of my eyes when I blind
and I slide.
I'm merely looking for traction
against the steely silence
of my empty gulps.
Then I pat my soul back
into my purse and go on my way.

Edward Walker

# DRIFTING THROUGH QUARTERS

Before sunrise couples
at small square tables
in Café Dumonde, mugs of coffee
and powdered beignets, where
night-worn men and dark-eyed women
sway their heads
like rats on the wharf scurry
alongside the Mississippi
a slight gleam of promise peeks
a red round face up east of Decatur

We seek not to take this precious
type of time too personal
kids grow each day
like you and I
and no matter
how hard we tried
we couldn't find a poet on Frenchmen
to raise us above the berm
take us someplace else
somewhere before before

# THE DAY AFTER SINATRA
# MARRIED MIA FARROW

So the coffee would stay hot all morning
Edna, the large-boned Dutch waitress,
her face and throat flushed from the heat
would first fill my thermos with boiling water
in the Circle Diner on Kutztown Road,
this July morning steamy and loud
with a highway crew at the counter,
two grizzled mailmen in the side booth
and us from the nearby construction site,
a job I loved for its noise and fresh air,
screwing big lag bolts into the sills
of Caloric Stove's new factory warehouse,
the whirr of the countersink drilling the wood,
clean white hemlock or spruce

and when one of the mailmen heads for the door
Edna calls out, *Hey Jack*
*how you think Frank's feeling this morning?*
Smoke from the grill and the cook's cigar
clouding the wide glass window:
Frank, 30 years her senior,
stepping from Sam Giancana's limo
or else whispering One For My Baby
into the spotlight: his death
in his voice with its flawless control,
his slanted fedora and raincoat,
his glittering life we could only imagine

though most of us are laughing by now
wolfing our hot cakes and eggs
when the old man yells back, *Tired as hell!*
pulling his hat down low at the door,
happy enough to be going to work

on a Friday under the dawnwashed sky
of Johnson's Great Society,
with the Lehigh Valley opening its thighs
and the week-end gorged with promise.

## LIFT COFFEE ROASTERS, WHITTIER

Double-shot glasses served on a plank,
one with a bubbling clearness that I
should take as Pellegrino, chaser
for my cortado. But I'm thinking
too much; the morning races electric,
clacks on my mind's ungreased tracks,
missing the connection between images—
my mental express's passenger stops
to let people into what I'm saying,
take a seat, maybe start a conversation.

In this roaster's red brick and mortar—
a place most recently a lowrider store;
before that, a women's clothing shop—
I can't get away from locomotives—
steel on steel's grind, tracks like DNA
before I was born. Neither can this town.
Freights ran Whittier Boulevard, loaded
with Sunkist crates of sweat and oranges
before Steinbeck, the Joads, any thought
that California was more than citrus.

My blood becomes not just invisible
but part of the scene, on a block
that's felt its own janglings, mortar
break, walls tumble. Maybe that's
what keeps me in Whittier. We stand
past our mutual earthquakes—for me
a divorce; some barely-paying jobs;
everyone making like trees and leaving,
their fallen promises skittering in wind;
years, like worn pavers, crack and fade.

Music rattles from the sound system—
something like calypso drums, or a glaring
of cats rummaging through empty cans.
I pull out my camera for a monochrome
instant of beat or noir—visual silkiness
akin to my cortado's mouth-feel—
slipping around solitude from the east
as it calls in full morning sun, a half-milk-
half-espresso stretch of shadows chased
with sips of soda water, a bite of voices

with my vegan coffee cake, low, pointed
my direction but addressed neither to me
nor to the barista—the Angeleno selfness
that sometimes gloms bubble to bubble,
sharing walls and angles till wind
and drift continues, by all means mutual
in the general direction of alone. Brick
voices mind their own walls and legacies,
while I sit in what passes for a station,
blocking steel wheels from my mind.

# ALONE IN THE CAFFE APPASSIONATO

On a bright day your eyes need time
to absorb the shadow
your ears, the hush

while coffee's aroma, too
grows slowly more nuanced
as you take it in

recognize a bean's mellow signature
a dash of hazelnut
or vanilla.

From the crowd outside rushing
to errand or food
few stop to enter this Old World

of mahogany
glass bowl
floral cushion:

three now at separate tables
sipping, reading, writing
under the blank stare

of Beethoven—stone bust
on a dark buffet—
past lover of coffee

whose passion remains only
in the code he left behind:
symphony, quartet...

the F minor sonata
its rumble building
to mountain thunder.

# NOTHING, TOO

*Love is built upon secrets, as lovely Venice upon invisible
and incorruptible piles in the sea.*
—Herman Melville, *Pierre, or The Ambiguities*

The courtyard is mine for now. And Venice.
The waiter has disappeared after pouring my coffee,
and the sparrows haven't alighted yet.

Is the Venice in my head less real
than a Venice past this stucco, these jasmined walls?
It too is a dream—a sunny one. It's all of yesterday
stilled in memory before a single sunbeam has reached
the shadowed quiet of my tablecloth.

I hear shutters clatter and turn in time to see
above me a young man, naked and lovely as he turns
again into a room, called back—as I imagine—
to his sweetheart's arms, unaware of me.

I hear a seagull and think of its brightness high up,
the wide mazes of its sunlit ways, its empty sky.
The mazes below—the water-lights, the echoes, facades
and empty mirrorings, insubstantial stone and labyrinths
of our dreams—they're nothing too, world's passing,

unless what was and is to be is, underneath it all,
one thing: love's primal Word, from darkness darkness'
necessary song forever sung.

Atop the opposite chair my first-arriving sparrow waits,
masked and flirty little thief that he is. I check around
for crumbs from yesterday.

## REDWOODS DINER

Hard to read the age of a stranger who calls everyone Honey.
She brings biscuits and gravy, Frisbee-sized pancakes, coffee
black as 45s. She laughed, a snort, when asked for a soy latté.
Her knee brace is the color of dishwater and droops at the
hinge. Her shoulders sag inside a long T-shirt, her brows into
parentheses. There's a story behind her eyes—let's say hissing
radiators and rusted swing sets, stern stepfather who threw her
out of the house, the childhood sweetheart lost to a hunting
accident. At a back table, she joshes the regulars, delivers pork
chops and hash browns. Somebody wants more maple syrup.
She limps toward the kitchen, whistles a familiar tune. I want
her to hum Hank Williams. I want to wash her apron.

## THE WAIT

Can I he pointed and of course
her hand replied smiling out
another coffee and otherwise
ignoring his all over her like
every yesterday and today
the same old thing but
what the hell she thought
what the hell her small tips
hung in the grinning balance

Angel Latterell

# BREAKFAST IN THE DETROIT AIRPORT ON THE WAY FROM SEATTLE

She doesn't know where you're from—only knows tired.

You are table six by the window.

Your red-eye fatigue is nothing—those two ton bags under
    her eyes
watched factories close here before the eggs got cold on your
    plate.

18 million persons served on their way to the sky in metal
birds no longer built in her town.

Maybe the one you flew in on was built by her husband.
Before the GATT toothed monster ate all the jobs.
Before she had to sling eggs at 5:00am in the airport.
Before the chicken laid the white oval you wasted not
knowing what *over easy* really meant.
Before the old man at the table next to you learned the
prayers he silently said to bless his ham.

The red tram flows above the airport diner leaving those who
    work here behind.

You watch this dance,
sip your cup of Joe
and do not fit in—
with your brand name coffee town and its fancy flourishing
    e-conomy.
If you had to drink the two-decade-old brown brew of
    abandonment,
dark as the souls simmered inside it,
you could taste Motor City.

# CAFÉS CHINOS

With Chinese letters that catch the eye
amid a multitude of Spanish signs
for pharmacies, photo shops, hardware stores
and offices, you find them discretely placed
on back streets downtown in the capital.
The words "*Café y comida china*" clarify
for those who don't know what to expect.
They are all almost alike with booths, chairs,
tables, a machine for espresso coffee behind
a counter lined with stools and an ancient
cash register at one end close to the door.
Store front windows let passersby glance
at sweet rolls of various shapes and the menu
of the day scribbled in Spanish on a small
blackboard showing a low price beneath the words
"*comida corrida.*" The personnel is also alike
from one cafe chino to another.
An oriental man with a gray fu manchu
stands behind the counter and stares
silently out into the street where
yet another day is passing. No one knows
exactly where he came from and when
but his hands say there was work
and his eyes say there was sorrow.
The aproned woman in the kitchen at the rear
where the scent of chop suey steams
must be his daughter, and the younger girl
who waits on tables must be hers.
All three carry out their chores in silence
except to speak to each other in a tongue
as chopped and indistinguishable as their food.
The woodwork isn't painted gold and red like
in the Chinese restaurants on Dolores Street.
There are no dragons painted on the ceilings,

no lanterns with dangling tassels;
only calendars, conventional family portraits
and an ordinary clock decorate the walls,
and time is sipped from thick glasses
of coffee with milk or cups of coffee alone.

James Miller Robinson

## CAFÉ LA HABANA IN MEXICO CITY

The old buildings on Bucareli
have housed the city's major newspapers
—*El Excelcior, El Universal, La Jornada, El Sol*—
through years of revolution, volcano, earthquake,
and the annual rains that flood the street over idle tires.
Café La Habana sits on the corner of Ayuntamiento
Avenue just as it has sat for over a century
with its half circle of counters, stools,
brass brewers, mahogany tables and chairs,
black and white photographic posters of the streets,
harbor, and *malecon* of old Havana
beneath which clients in Mexico can gaze
with nostalgia as they eat, sip coffee, and talk
about the sad situations of the country and the world.

It is the kind of place where Carlos Fuentes
and García Márquez met over a stack of open pages,
plates, saucers, cups, and discussed how there is
nothing more surreal and absurd than the daily news,
other tables occupied then by reporters,
correspondents, editors, printers, journalists,
and politicians. At another table in this very room
a young Che sat with Fidel and Raúl over *tortas*
and *tostones* to mark out the delivery of the island
to the people of its fields, drawing lines on a map
as cigar smoke intermingled with the aroma
of roasted coffee that remains today.
                                        The empty tables
have now grown to outnumber the occupied
—so many *compañeros* kidnapped, killed or disappeared.

Stephen J. Kudless

# IN WATERSTONE'S BOOKS: LONDON, JULY

It's a big shop,
The one on the corner
Near the university in Bloomsbury.
There's a Costa Coffee bar upstairs,
Where people like us can hide
Behind open pages and scribbled notes.
Sitting there, with my dark Arabica (Grande),
And you with your pot of tea,
We made for a curious pair of bookworms,
Talking about Lorca (your favorite), Pinter,
And perhaps even Stoppard.
The words "post-modern" and "surrealism"
Mixed with our beverages and biscuits
As naturally as sugar and lemon.
I couldn't understand why you put cream in your tea;
You thought black coffee was barbaric.
We agreed though, that in matters of more than taste,
Some things, like people, did not seem to fit together,
But they simply do.
Then the talk returned to Lorca.

# MUGS

It takes me until our fourth day in Puerto Rico to realize
I should have been ordering café con leche every morning,
milk heated to add to the rich dark coffee.
We only have one more morning left in Fajardo, so
I have to take my café con leche habit home. July.
August. September the hurricane hits,
CNN reporter in the lobby of our resort, windows blown out,
trees the last resistance of this furious weather.
They must have brought the pool furniture inside,
must have given indoor cages to the outdoor parrots,
must have stopped the funicular from its angled climb up
and down. Our room was at the bottom, looking out
on the little harbor, the ocean a few yards away, almost
at our feet. They wouldn't have left anyone stranded.
Our first day I went up on the funicular, into the spa.
The woman asked politely, professionally, if I had any questions:
what, I asked, is that gorgeous tree outside? She laughed.
That's the *flamboyan*, she said. Her parents had had a farm
up on the mountainside, and her mother had planted flamboyans
near the patio. The trees blossomed orange (like outside
the spa), red, and her mother somewhere had found purple.
She missed the patio. I walked out of the spa and looked
up into the branches and blossoms of the flamboyant tree.
Against the wind, these things sustain us: blossoms, coffee,
the memory of what's lost, the drive to rebuild.

# BARS AND BEGGARS:
# LAS RAMBLAS, BARCELONA

1
You'd hardly notice her at first,
might even step aside

when she passes, what with warnings
pickpockets and bag thieves.

She shuffles by
rattles her cup—its voice pure need—

tired coat-threads, reddened hands,
a face of centuries.

You remember her shoes
once black—now lamentable—

Needles of rain catch silvered hair
soak her shoes.

2
Café tables no bigger than trays buzz
with caffeinated chatter—

business, gossip stirred in sipped espresso,
my hands around a steaming cup when the old woman scuffs in.

Coins rest in her open hand like an offering,
so small a weight.

Moments of calculation, and she turns away,
her eyes hold not one bit of hope.

Though she asks for nothing,
and I have planned less

I speak fractured Spanish, *¿Quiere qué, señora?*
*Café con leche, por favor*—

Something like a smile passes over her face.
*Con leche* she repeats.

Shirley J. Brewer

## HOMELESS MAN OUTSIDE WALGREEN'S
*Baltimore, MD*

The day before the blizzard
he sits cross-legged on cold concrete
next to a trash can, a gray
blanket loose around his shoulders.

He holds up a homemade sign. Wait,
he doesn't have a home.
I give him a dollar and a smile.
*Thanks, angel,* he says.

Sir, if I were an angel
I'd whisk you off to a Greek
Paradise where gray is banned.
Instead, we find this diner that serves
breakfast all day. Over pancakes,

we talk about city life. You call
Freddie Gray your brother, never mind
the different shades of your skin.
You are kin, in the unruly way
layers of circumstance pile up

like a thousand gray blankets. Change
begins one exchange at a time.
We signal for the waitress
to refill our coffee cups.

# BERKELEY: YOUTH AND AGE

Winter cabbages blooming in pots
In front of banks and restaurants,
The fashion in Berkeley, it's just like New York,
The world grows smaller and more reassuring,
All this purple and green leafiness
To supplement brokers and panhandlers,
Or do I merely mean more ornamental
While far less reassuring? Now I watch
The delivery man from the bakery van
Flirt with a fellow at the corner table
of the Caffe Strada, once the Mediterranean.
—Hey, weren't you going to talk to me?
—Sure, I thought you were delivering.
The van man sports a torn sweatshirt, grey
Dirt on his cheekbone, a greying Errol Flynn
Mustache, and witty mannerisms
Half homoerotic, half old jock.
The grad student, with chiseled cleancut Frank Merriwell
Features and a massive Saint Bernard
Solid and calm as library paneling
Strolling remotely among the tables,
Is wealthier and younger, therefore used
To being the object of resentful flirtation
To which he responds with good manners
As he was bred; including a slight edge.
Younger man—You've kept your weight down.
Older man—I'm still the stud I was.
Hey, is that your dog?
(Said intermittently with a variety
of inflections.—Hey, is that your *dog*?
Hey, is that *your* dog? Is *that* your dog?)
Youth slips a glance of resignation
Across the round table at his companion,
Another clean youngster, who just at present

Is concentrating on his croissant and napkin.
The van man grins to show his canine teeth
And try another cadence.
—Buddy, can I *buy* your *dog?*

Natasha Kochicheril Moni

# WE HAVE BEEN HERE BEFORE

i.

To explain we are in a café seems
redundant.

                You with your striped
          shirt, all collar and cotton

and the dog who follows
all drool and collarless.

You could have named him
          by now, a thousand

Rexes or Suzanne after your first
girlfriend—but who names a dog

for that?—except you,
you are present without fur

          (it is sunny
          after all) and the light

through the window
through glasses makes you think

               of water but not really
               water—

the sensation
of rocking

               which brings you to this moment
               where the woman beside the frosted

brownies turns—you spy her, the girl
from high-school, twenty years more

      sunrise on her face, hair still fallen
      wheat, a tan line filling the gap where a ring

must have been and you speak of reunions
while the barista prepares your drink from memory.


ii.

You offer me the world
on the counter by the window, the world
a flat cookie raised with more sugar
than the world may hold, steal
the Northern hemisphere with your teeth.


iii.

Here, I decline your offer for cake—even though I have
been wanting it. Because you have brought me the world,
I will eat the South while you tap out the rhythm
of desire on the edge of my plate. The ocean
becomes my tongue, land shipwrecked on lips.


iv.

Is there such a thing as too much metaphor—extended?
Does the world rest in us, our mouths the entry?

v.

You ask what happened to the dog and I respond *Dog?*
The truth is I have always wanted a parakeet, no,
not parakeet, hedgehog. Besides, the dog is over
there wagging and it is, beside the tree where
the children climb like monkeys in spring. Look
and you will see them now. The one nearest the dirt,
scraping nails where bark should be.

## OVER LATTÉS

am I going to understand this poem she said
    watching the rain pour
    down outside the window
    as they prepared to leave
    the cafe after an hour or so
    of small talk while avoiding
    the slightly disturbing lightning
    or at least getting soaked
because you know she said
    with both the double-espresso hit
    and her blue-gray eyes unsettling him
    still even after all these years
    while she set down her empty cup
    on the green faux-marble table top
I never understood all that strange stuff you wrote
    she started to put on her sensible
    ankle-length black or maybe
    just dark blue wool coat
    while he stood there waiting
    for those recalled years or at least
    the rain outside to finish its work
and you an English major all those years ago
    he laughed setting down his cup too
    when they were all California sun and 70s-soaked
    at Cal-Santa Cruz loving at cummings
    lowercase intensity and ferlinghetti's too
    and reading Sexton and Plath's terrible
    power to give nightmare beauty
but I knew it had to be about me then and you
    so they could have been hanging out
    at this same coffee shop too only now the
    music's so damn different one of them
    had to be thinking or wanted to say
    meeting anyway accidentally like this

do you still write about me she smiled a little
    they both imagined how their worlds
    had imagined them so completely since
    they were almost through the opened door
    back out into the rain both continuing
    now gone yes or maybe never gone.

## COFFEE WITH NAOMI

In his staked-out seat
by a front window
at Starbucks this morning,
an elderly man sips coffee
as he reads from an anthology—
"Bill's Beans," by Naomi Shihab Nye:
*I don't know how deep bean roots go.*
*We could experiment.*
A young girl outside, four or so,
flowered pink blouse,
blue bib overalls
brakes her skip long enough
to flatten her face against
his window.
She lets out a squeal and     smacks it
hard     with a wet kiss.
The girl's mother snatches her away
uprooting a short-lived moment
of enchantment     leaving the window
which could have been
the old man's cheek
aglow with moisture.
*They go deep,* he says to Naomi,
*the roots go very deep.*

# THE PLAGIARIZER OF WORDS

Out of the streaming radio of voices in the café,
out of the sports section spread before him
on the tiny round table they stick you with at Peet's,
out of Dunn's *New and Selected Poems 1974-1994*
obscuring the scores, not to mention
the junk drawer in the dresser of his head,

he snitches words like a frog snatching flies:
   *thimble  haphazard  numbskull*
which collage themselves like Rockettes which
sets him off on:
   *collision  kalashnikov*
the syllables wiggling and kicking in his mouth
next to the hazelnut muffin.

Before long he finds himself ventriloquizing
(so as not to seem too crazy to those around):
   *garaggge  zzzhivago  jjje ne sais quoi*
his coffeed head now kazooing like a dozen bees
which in turn brings him back to: *numbskull.*

The air is reverent with fraudulence, fraudulent
with reverie! He loves splashing about in language,
bucket in hand, toeing the debris.
From Dunn this morning he pockets:
   *jetty  pucker  obstinate*

Flipping back then to the live program around him:
   *fidget  swivel  potluck*
He thinks what a stew it all is, and how plucky his Bubby,
a girl back in Romania peeling turnips, wiping her hands
on a coarse brown apron. Then strolling out,
smuggled under his breath:
   *babushka  babussshka  ba-busssssh-ka*

Sharon MacFarlane

## COFFEE ROW

There are only two hundred and forty people
in our prairie town.
The school will close when the enrolment sinks
below seventy.
It will mean the death of our village.
If new people move in everyone's first question is
"Do you have school-age kids?"

Every Tuesday morning women meet for coffee
at Ken's Kafe.
Ten or twelve squeeze in together at one table,
workers from the village office and the credit union
and retired grandmothers in their seventies and eighties.

We discuss world events but local news is more important.
When Mabel announces that her daughter is pregnant,
we all raise our steaming mugs of coffee in celebration.
Another child for kindergarten five years down the road!

# GROWING UP, ONE CUP AT A TIME

The coffee is weak at the local diner.
It has to be after sitting on the warmer plate for hours.
The pots are never empty, except at night
when they've been swirled
with salt and a wedge of lemon.
Stains removed. Evidence gone.
Not really coffee anyway.

Bottomless cups at Denny's.
Bitter brew made harsher with cigarettes and self-important talk.
The lack of *Focus* as we dream up our *Stunts*.
Caffeine mainlined as our drug of choice.
Sometimes a dollar is all we have to get a fix.
And we're better than these circumstances anyway.

Styrofoam cups in hospital waiting rooms.
Before Styrofoam was killing the ozone.
Before bad things could happen to us.
This pain isn't ours. It belongs to old people. Other people.
Poke a hole in the Styrofoam cup.
Let the real worries fall through.
Snap off the top rim in small nervous pieces.
This isn't happening to us. It's happening to someone else.
We're just a lipstick stain on the white cup of cold brown liquid.
It's not really happening anyway.

Dunkin Donuts has a drive-thru.
The coffee is strong, tasty, smells of faraway places.
They'll sell you a large cup
and you can use it to keep alert on the drive.
The drive to somewhere else: somewhere more real;
somewhere less real.
Somewhere no one knows you; or they know the real you.
Behind the wheel of your father's expensive cast-off

you drink your coffee and drive.
To Evanston or Rockford. To Paris or Shanghai.
To Sumatra or Arabia. Or back home.
It's just a cup of coffee anyway.

The Starbucks opens.
Coffee becomes culture, ordering an art form.
It's better coffee, worth the money—
the kind of coffee that elevates you.
But it's not the coffee of your youth. It's posing.
Hiding behind soy whips and half shots.
Telling you that if you drink it you will be welcome
in the crowd of fellow coffee drinkers,
changing the coffee shop from a place of black-clad iconoclasts
to a club with punch cards and Wi-Fi.
And that's not coffee anyway.

Chanel Brenner

# TO THE FRUSTRATED MOTHER
# IN STARBUCKS WITH HER
# THREE-YEAR-OLD SON

Don't worry. One day, he will
stop hitting you when he's mad,
hands swatting at your face,
like a short-circuited robot.

He will stop throwing himself
on floors, and thrashing
his head like a punk rocker,
when you tell him, No.

Some day, he will stop
running outdoors every time
he sees a mangy pigeon,
bobbing along the sidewalk,

leaving you to spill coffee,
and chase him, grabbing
his shirt, just before he steps
into moving traffic.

You probably won't notice
when he stops. You'll be
too busy, helping him trace
his upper-case letters, playing

game after game of Roshambo,
listening to his knock-knock jokes.
You'll be too busy answering
his questions, *Mommy,*

*can I tell you something?*
*Mommy, can I have gummy bears?*

*Mommy, who was the first*
*person on earth?*

You probably won't remember
how you thought it would be easier
when he turned three,
but it wasn't.

You won't remember,
till you see another mother,
with her three-year-old—
her jaw tense, her hand

clutching his arm
too tightly, as he grabs
and pulls her hair
with his freakishly strong fist.

Then you will remember,
how you wanted to escape,
how you thought
it would never end.

By then, your son will be standing still
in line beside you, ordering Iced Caramel Macchiato,
his large hands hanging at his sides.
Then, you will remember

him small in your lap,
one hand holding your finger,
the other pointing at a balloon,
*Mommy, Boom!*

# IN DUNKIN' DONUTS WITH
# MY MOTHER

What was I thinking when I took her with me
to drink hot macchiato? Seeing the price,
my mother asks if I'm the Queen of Sheba.
Waving my wildflower guide like a semaphore,
she points to a picture of young chicory leaves
that color Morgan Point's marsh. Tomorrow,
my mother will uproot and pot chicory stems
in my cellar, teach me to roast and grind roots
to stretch out coffee. She's proud of pinching
pennies I won't stoop to pick up, brags how
chicory got her through the morning when
the egg money ran out. To distract her, I ask
about growing up in Kentucky, being in love.
More chicory. Called *Blue Sailors*, the flower
sprang up where a maiden died waiting for her
love to return from the Pacific. No transplanting,
chicory made up its own mind like my father
whose eyes were wild, brave blue as the weed.
Always hungry for her coffee, her biscuits, letting
her know he was coming from the barn to wash up
for breakfast, Daddy's whistle ribboned the wind.

Karen Klassen

## ALL FOR FREE

Unless I am at McDonalds where
I can have an apple pie with hot coffee
and not too expensive I don't like to eat out
specially when it is costing so much and all I can see
is the price and no salad bar.

But once in a while, the ladies are getting
together to have a lunch at Uncle Willy's
and there they have a very nice buffet
and a salad bar with all different sorts.

Then you don't have to wait for them to come
once to ask for your drinks and then again
for your order and then to bring it and
again to see if it's good. That takes me
too long.

But now, it is very in style to go out just for
coffee. I don't know what all the fuss is
about Starbucks. Everyone going there
all the time, me and Ika thought we would
too, but when we are in line and see that
one small coffee is $3.45 we looked at each other
and said, *Na! For that price we can buy
a whole jar Nescafe.*

We walked out and went straight to her house
and had hot instant coffee with brown buns
and jam and a warmed up *Plushke*
all for free.

## MCDONALDS, INDIANA, PA.
## JANUARY 2009

In the room, the old talk about the dead.
Grandfathers dribble hot coffee down wrinkled chins,
Mumble on about insulin and diabetes.

One grandfather takes two creams in his coffee,
A ritual started sixty-eight years ago
In the morning on some Wisconsin farm.
He speaks of the loved ones he's buried
As if they're pennies he's lost.

He speaks of faith.

In the room,
A girl, too young for the bulbous belly
Below her greased stained apron,
Sweeps the floor and talks about her daughter
Riding the bus for the first time that year.

She speaks to a shell of a man in a WWII hat.
He smiles, pretending to listen.
He remembers being 19
And so surprised by the size of the tread on a tank,
And how he thought then
That it must make accordions of everything it rolled over,
Even men.

On my table
There is a cup of coffee no longer steaming.

Outside, there's a field of snow,
Mostly undisturbed.

# CAFE CILANTRO HAVEN
*winter storm Grayson, January 2018*

at home the furnace struggles to warm to the sixties
so instead of building a fire I choose to be here
few others have braved this bombogenesis storm

I sit away from the door   warmed by hot coffee
an arctic cold front commands the dark evening streets
the lighted icicles trimming the window welcome

at home the main drain is frozen solid
neither boiling salt water   heater   or snake will fix it
so precious the toilet here   clean and high

three teen-aged girls chat by the window
a couple is tentative as if new to each other
a solitary teacher sips coffee nearby

I thank him for his project   laying name stones
in front of homes where slaves once lived in Guilford
he's hoping to spread the practice to other towns

surrounding wall photos are red   blue and yellow
welcome color after black sky and white snow of the Green
I glory in this *hygge* cafe moment

'what's that ballad playing?' I ask the cashier
—a 90's song from before he was born—
he checks in back   replies *'Now and Forever'*

## COFFEE BREAK

We needed to talk, colleague and I.

He suggested we meet for tea.
I agreed if there was coffee.

Somewhere relaxing. Not overly noisy.
Where work-related discussion can prevail
for topics we wanted to nail.

We found a café. They took our first names.
Called us when drinks were ready to take.

I stirred honey into vanilla bean latté.
He lost himself in steamy blueberry infusion.

"How's your tea?" I asked. "Strong? Weak?
Do you like the flavor?"

"It's tea," he answered nonchalantly.

We sipped and listened to bluesy jazz.
Lifted our heads to gaze at landscapes mounted
on walls. Smiled upon hearing newsy gossip.
Notepads at our elbows, unopened.
Cell phones positioned atop.

Drinks finished. Our break on the brink
of finishing. We untethered ourselves from
relaxation and together raced back to the office.

I forgot what we needed to discuss.
He was amiss for he too had forgotten.

Meeting justified, if only for one reason.
I needed coffee and he couldn't forego tea.

# DRIVING TO MY FIRST
# DAY OF THERAPY

A therapist might be a pry bar
to open up the past again,
focusing searchlights on my apocrypha,
the untidy, strived-for milestones,

the scarf and gloves of my heart's cold hungers.
Some days it was easy for me to be steamed
into froth by an argument with a co-worker
over artificial sweeteners. December
is such a gaudy time of year. Poinsettias
on the window sills at Starbucks reach

their leafy peak and the Christmas cactus
on the counter, showing wounds.
We're all wounded in some way.
That frowning tattooed guy who,

as we're inching forward in line, keeps
a three-foot gap, is wounded.
And the patchouli-scented girl, wearing
a paisley skirt and kerchief, wounded.
Sometimes I get stuck in the tinsel-flicker
of decision. Which brew to choose?

Sumatra. Java. Kona. Or which therapist?
Surely the one I've chosen won't be contemptuous
of poetry or anything wispy, anything
that flutters in the webbing of the breath.

## KNOWN THINGS

       She steps back
into spring air, after
the doctor has said *lumps*
and
*yes, lumps,*
and
*don't worry*
*yet,* and *most likely*    *nothing.*

And she is drifting
forward, nowhere
to stand, nothing
known but this mid-morning
light, green
tendrils pushing up
through grey snow along the sidewalk,
a line of children
crossing toward the museum, hands linked
in a chain.

She finds herself
following, finds herself
in the overpriced café, holding
a latte.
How pleasing, the blue porcelain mug
curving warm against her palms. How
pleasing, a round table
by a window,
an extravagant scone. Sunlit
cars glinting past. People's
faces.
The flicks and darts of brown
in bare bushes—sparrows,

how they fly
through shadow, light,
shadow,
light.

Alexis Rhone Fancher

# FOR THE SAD WAITRESS AT
# THE DINER IN BARSTOW

beyond the kitchen's swinging door,
beyond the order wheel and the pass-through piled
high with bacon, hash browns, biscuits and gravy,

past the radio, tuned to 101.5-FM
*All Country - All the Time,*
past the truckers overwhelming the counter,
all grab-ass and longing.

in the middle of morning rush you'll
catch her, in a wilted pink uniform,
coffee pot fused in her grip, staring over
the top of your head

you'll follow her gaze, out the fly-specked, plate
glass windows, past the parking lot,

watch as she eyes those 16-wheelers barreling
down the highway, their mud guards
adorned with chrome silhouettes of naked women
who look nothing like her.

the cruel sun throws her inertia in her face.
this is what regret looks like.

maybe she's searching for that hot day in August
when she first walked away from you.

there's a choking sound
a semi makes, when it pulls off the
highway; that downshift a death rattle
she's never gotten used to.

maybe she's looking for a way back.
maybe she's ready to come home.

(But for now) she's lost herself
between the register and the door, the endless
business from table to kitchen, she's

as much leftover as those sunny side eggs,
yolks hardening on your plate.

## JUST COFFEE, PLEASE

We met, as I remember, at that sketching group,
exchanging pleasantries, including where we worked,
as we circled the hired model for proper view.

At any rate, all hippied up
you sauntered in the diner where I worked
and plopped down at my counter.
Then, as if I had unlevered
a trick pail of water suspended just above your seat,
lost all the bluster that you entered with,
stuttered and blurted a coffee order while petitioning a movie date
all in one breath.
Perhaps it was my starched pink uniform, its little apron,
or that my untamed hair was tucked inside a cap,
but there you sat, blowing on your coffee,
blowing steam,
and me handling my customers while trying to explain to you
that I was spoken for
then had to watch with my pasted waitress smile
as you struggled with the protocol of a decent exit,
to leave a tip or not on a social visit,
and for just a coffee after all, okay a dime,
and swiveled off your stool while my regulars smirked
and you ran wham! into the spotless closed glass doors
of the Powell Street B and G
across from Woolworth's at the cable turnaround.
        Blood spouted from your nose.
Bud, the boss, leapt from behind his stove
nabbed the first-aid-kit in a one-armed swoop.
Minor pandemonium as he tried to blot your face
when all you wanted was to get away.
Which you finally managed.
Plastic butterflies, or were they ladybugs,
adorned the doors of B and G next day.

I hope your next excursion had more grace
and more success. I hope you found a graceful lady.

I was hiding in me then a sort of seed with ears.
Today he's edging sixty.

I hope the lady's with you now.

Jessica Cory

# AWKWARD SOCIAL ANXIETY POEM

I fear visiting the sidewalk cafe
settled near the banks of the Thames,
expect that the salad will be slightly wilted or hot
tea a spot too chilled; I wouldn't want
to ruin the perfect image by dropping my fork,
its clink-clinking from brick sidewalk to leaf
pile to rest in the gutter, awaiting the next rainfall.

Should the shoreline be muddy, the sky nimbus-
scattered, or should "Kind of Blue" sprinkle
from the pianist's slender fingers instead of "Sketches of Spain,"
this grand illusion would emerge an artifice.

Yes, safety should come first, and my comfort zone
forgoes rosé (which isn't served here anyway),
guards against the barista's curious glance, his hands
wielding a medium skim-milk mochachino,
as he saunters toward the overstuffed red velour sofa
Scrabble and I have claimed in the absence of British rivers.

## ONE WEEK AFTER

Right now, a bakery café manager
is disciplining an employee in Spanish.
Though I can't speak the language,
the tone of her voice
breaks my heart.

The employee's head is down,
staring at her shoes,
her fingers are knotted behind her back
like her long dark braid,
that swings ever so subtly.

Can one dropped tray of cinnamon buns
matter on September 18th, 2001?

My coffee is scorching my hand
through the thin cardboard cup.
I force myself to hold on,
carry it to the table by the window
not wanting to miss the human parade.

Young women pass by in every
shade and attire of lovely,
making me sorry each time
to be female, middle-aged, unbeautiful.
The sun has a way of turning
those women into glowing orchids
Georgia O'Keefe would envy.

Men, far less glittery,
amble or stride by my window.
One man, wide-carriaged,
slight limp in his gait,

holds to the odd-angled path
the planes the Cambridge Marriot
make of the plaza.

He's nearly bald, full-bearded,
I can see only the side of his face.
I imagine it's my ex-husband
of a dozen years ago.
I've the sudden urge to run after him,
throw my arms around him,
kiss his cheek,
even if it's not him.

But the hot coffee is welded to my hand
as I am to the red plastic chair.
If I did go, he'd either choke me or laugh,
wiping away the poison of my kiss
whether or not it was my ex.

In a little while I'll be sitting in a classroom
filled with poets who persevere at
making sense of the world with words on paper,
words read aloud.

Today it seems we're all trying to call out
through bandaged mouths,
scream through layers of plaster and ash.

Words can't fell two towers—
beliefs fused to the underside of
language do,
speeding through neurotransmitter roadways
in our brains trying to make the green,
to get there before the light turns.

All of the words want to be
in the front of the line,
all want to be first to arrive.

But all of the words are sacred,
like *god* and *bless* and *America*
and *coffee* and *sorry* and *gracias*,
but not necessarily in that order.

Ellaraine Lockie

# IN THE PRIVACY OF PUBLIC

Two women sit silent
surrounded by the clamor of the coffee shop
Matching shades of sandy blonde hair
The same sea-green eyes
Except the younger pair
stare through rims red as coral
into some far-off horizon
The light in them drowned

Beacons in the older set
Her hand stretched
across the table stroking the other woman's
folded arm that holds up her chin
Only one blink when saltwater eyes
are dabbed with a napkin

The ice in one glass has melted
Coffee across from it would be cold
Yet the rubbing does not ebb
Something horrible here that can be alluded to
only through an umbilical cord
And perhaps only in the privacy of public

## GOING FOR COFFEE AFTER AN
## AL-ANON MEETING

To get through each day,
I kill my husband, Sandy says.
I imagine him driving home
through the night silence
of a blizzard, wipers clicking
back and forth clogging with snow.
Blinded, he crashes through a guard rail
plummeting 200 feet into a ravine.
Then there is the funeral. I go
all out looking fantastic,
dabbing my eyes and pouting
in my new black dress.
I already have it hanging
in the closet and I'm dieting
for the fatal occasion, she adds
while twisting her foot round
like a cat flicking her tail.
Lynette confesses, I've been praying
for lightning to strike.
My husband is on our tin roof
replacing flashing around the chimney
when a thunderbolt rockets him
into our neighbors' hedges,
his last sip of Jack Daniel's dribbling
down his chin. And, yes
I too have the black dress.
I got it at Bergdorf's.
How can he complain about the $1,200
price tag when it's for his funeral?
Cheryl admits, I actually almost killed
my husband once—I was so furious
I knocked him out with the vacuum hose.

If you try this,
you should use a steel hose—
those plastic ones
won't do a goddamned thing.

Laura Ring

## TO THE BARISTA AT THE SACRED GROUNDS ESPRESSO

A drunk can only love one thing but I want
to love you. I swallow it all, cup
after sinless cup. Sit here with my no booze,
no smokes. Suffer salvation piped through the vents.

Church girls love everyone so no one's special.
You, Barista, you hate me a little—
fix an eye-for-an-eye on my tar-dipped nails,
spike my joe with brimstone. Go ahead,

pour me another from your god-stung lips—
your words are bells, a barkeep's Last Call.
Tell me again—yes, the water for wine.
The part where my cup runneth over.

Kevin Zepper

## CUP OF TWILIGHT

She floats through the Universe Coffee Hut and orders a tall, dark cup of twilight. A Mercury Comet carries her to the beach by the bay; she spreads her shawl on the ground where grass and sand blur. It is early a.m., her favorite time, when the fiery yellow sun and shy, coy moon exchange glances in the pale iris sky. She sips the spangled twilight slow, pausing when she's connecting with something, as she does in the morning. The ocean air, rolling in from a point where the only land is underneath deep water, cools her face, dissipates the remaining steam from her open cup, fluttering breath from a blue mother. For her, all of the elements in her life melt like a sandcastle; magic surrounds her. She warms her hands on the wax cup, feels the honeycomb dimples on the amber wrap holder, savoring each swallow down to the bitter brown. In this moment, the sky clock winds down and balance regenerates. After she empties her cup, she gazes into the bottom; tiny stars shimmer among earthy dregs.

## SPIN

The superheroes have arrived, slipping in
on the Polar Front. They've been saving up
for this day—disaster looms. The town
is busy, pork chops are on discount, and
everyone is buying the diversion.

The tragedy will be averted and private
economic freedom guaranteed. Your
personal information will be safe. With us.
By sundown, all the traitors will be hung
like garlic.

In disguise, I sip dark coffee in a throwaway
restaurant. The corner is crowded
with laptops reading faces. Eyes are dead
alert. My costume itches a little—it is
underneath and coloured for power.

A child winks at me across her mocca sweet
and nearly discloses my secret. But she
is discreet and I am saved, free to pursue
my mission.

When the waitress arrives I tell her I am
not one of them—I am a different kind, I
stress. She nods and gets me a refill,
leaves the bill.

I pay, looking up at the cameras. I now
have 360 degree global vision. As
I take control.

With my identity protected, I beam down
the Prime Meridian to the target. I secretly

thank the camera operators—they have
secured the spin with mass exhilaration.

All the sensitive information is in a chip
that will pass through the eye
of the needle. I manufacture a nick
of time. Tomorrow, The Pope will announce
a miracle.

## ASK ALBERT

When and if squared,
divided by maybe,
and if the probability of maybe
is less than fifty percent,
the answer is never
The equation flows
from young Einstein's lips
to my ears as we lunch
in...it is it Berlin or Vienna
or New York or Princeton?
"What is never," I wonder;
"Ah," the genius replies,
"that is the challenge..."
"If I cannot define never,
then quantum mechanics,
the theory of relativity
surely lie beyond my ken."
He sips tea,
served European style,
the amber flew floating
in a glass resting
within a silver holder;
I delight in my muscular
Vietnamese coffee,
an addiction birthed
during tumultuous times
A waiter brings
fat, garlicky sausages,
wedges of cheese, some blue-veined,
others flecked with caraway
"It is not the best of times,"
Einstein proclaims,
"but neither is it the wurst."
I flick an ember of my cigarette

into the metal ash tray
whose faded rim once
announced the cafe's name...
Camels, unfiltered, my choice
before I rescued my lungs;
The young Einstein puffs
on his Meerschaum,
its white clay bowl
bearing the face of Beethoven,
the sweet smoke
drifting upward toward
the unnamed air
into which Einstein vanishes
(Did he really smoke a pipe?
I must check that out)
"When and if squared,
divided by maybe,
and if the probability of maybe
is less than fifty percent,
the answer is never."
She is puzzled
as I am befuddled
"What is never?"
Any number of possibilities...
"Ask Albert...
He's an amiable fellow...
He bought lunch."

Caroline N. Simpson

## GHOST ALLEY ESPRESSO

Perched behind the window we peer
like owls watching all who enter
the shadow before our corner
café. From above, they wander
down cobblestones, turn at the sewer,
search each doorway for a specter.
Finding none, they litter
the walls with gum of every color,
depart the alley to recover
daylight. At our counter
we sip coffee and decipher
—swiveling our heads, a typewriter—
the left behind rainbow letter.

Michael Ugulini

# TAKE OUT COFFEE AT MIDNIGHT

The diner kitchen sings its Florida song
A respite for the beachgoers soaked with sun
A place where all who come feel they belong
They savor take-out fare—pay up—and run

When midnight comes, a whole new crowd slips in
They're living for tonight, and so they should
They may not ever come this way again
They're staking throwaway claims of where they stood

Tomorrow they will board their planes for home
Or pile in cars and leave the Coast behind
The wily surf will still rise up and foam
Not offering them the permanent ties that bind

The coffee crowd is lined up out the door
Their eyes are asking diner staff for more

The rain has stopped and there's time, between storms, for a walk downtown. Rainbows marble the oil-stained streets, and light strung in the sycamores hover like a brilliant cloud. It's dusk, and as you turn toward a cafe, you throw your hand out to shield a boy from the passing cars, but the boy isn't there. You order coffee. The cup is warm in your hands, and you can see your breath hanging in the cold air. The lights at the end of the street are brighter now in the growing dark. They seem to swarm and pulse. They're so beautiful, and for a moment, you think, unendurable, but they're not.

# ii.

# Home Grounds

*I went out the kitchen to make coffee—yards of coffee.*
*Rich, strong, bitter, boiling hot, ruthless, depraved.*
*The life blood of tired men.*

—Raymond Chandler

Katharyn Howd Machan

## FRIDAY, COFFEE

and my notebook on our porch,
you asleep upstairs, midnight husband,
our son on my pillow

here alone sun starts a path
of light and sound in morning's
reach, my cotton skirt a sky

across my page the smallest
crimson spider finds her frantic
way to safety, disappears

how long have you and I
made home each other,
words of longing coupled rhyme?

I sip again, taste cream
and sugar full and sweet
in caffeine's quiet roar

the moment holds—and then
Benjamin in his new pajamas
crows joy at the open door

Jane Blanchard

new brew of coffee
filtering through the morning
melting mental frost

## CONSUMED

It wakes before me,
it rumbles and stirs,
scratches itself in anticipation
and stretches, the night's inaction away.
The light comes in through the window
falling on the empty gold coaster,
it's carved marble shining,
longing to fulfill its purpose.
My husband is still sleeping,
his eye mask hiding
his desires from the world
and mine, driving me out
to touch the cold floor.
I walk directly to the coffee pot.
This is what it has waited for all night.
My deep longing,
for just that moment, when
the flavors of Sumatra mixed
with just a touch of milk, frothed
cold,
touch my lips.
Everything stops.
I am consumed, engulfed and cease to exist
in this resonating eternity.

Tom Hansen

# BEFORE DAYLIGHT

to finger-skim hallway
to dead-reckon room
dark streaming through you around you
to squat by dim coals
and blow last night's fire back to life
to brew too much coffee too strong

to raise a steaming cup in salute
to the fire to the room
full of flickering light
to darkness again doomed to die
in the birth of the half-light of day
to your own little sanctum
of midnight somewhere within—

steeped in this richness to sip
black acrid fire from your cup
*God this hurts! How I love it!*
as afterburn blossoms
sweet flower of pain
searing its name on your tongue

## COFFEE

Morning coaxes, cold
one cup and thought

at a time from bones.
No milk or sugar

but undiluted quiet
from a stove's burners,

a phantom clock
once on a white wall

above my chair
and the black comfort

that calls remembrance
past a red eye,

brewing
through the dullness,

regrets and missed lives.
I turn to it

for warmth
on days only it touches me.

We are so alike—
cooling, then tepid,

left with a dark ring
and spent grounds.

## COFFEE PSALM

Hard as beetles or wood, but cleaved
like Buddha's eyes, coffee beans
pour from the foil pouch, rain sound

on round stones or heaps of drying grain.
How I will wake—taken by steam, I believe,
but first the machine buzz I hold against me.

*Dampen the grind. Wake no one*
*but me. I want to be this morning alone,*
*for now, to see something there I miss.*

The blades are sharp, the grounds soft
like sugar, but dark. They leave residue
on my finger as I touch the blade to skin,

to tap the last black crumbs from the edge.
I crave it too soon with its scent, hear water
puff, sizzle, spit as it pours. Dawn fills

the windows, pushes at the screens.
The trees inflate with green light outside.
Kitchen lights, dull florescent, flicker like boredom

or delirium. I am wishing a dog would bark,
wishing for someone to honk a horn, yell out.
Lao Tzu loved the empty cup, useful, clean

volume of air, tucked inside the clay, so cool.
He did not revel the filling as I do, hot coffee,
like melted glass torn, molasses brown,

until I tilt and lift, and it cuts, finished, just once,
cup's usefulness in being full and waiting
to be empty. I pull the vapor, feel it blown

white through lung and vein, taste heat, sour dark,
at the base of my tongue. Two sips in, nothing
will stop the day from coming, nothing

will lead me to lie down in the coiled sheets,
to find the sleep again, my eyes shriveled tight
as damp cloves. I drink now and let the words

come to suspend me, waving from stinging wires,
to slide me into the tart hours when I face you,
when I will open my mouth to say it—

the black steam, the empty cup inside, the hum.

## MORNING ROUNDS

He gets up first, makes
the coffee while she lets
her dreams come to no
end. He feeds the dogs,
two cups for the big one,
one cup for the pup. She
likes coffee with cream.
He is retired. She goes
to work, brings home
the endless stress of
colleagues convinced
that family and the next
door neighbors keep
them from seeing
the evening stars or
the weekend's clear air.
He will deadhead the flowers,
carry out the dead mole
the cats fought over during
the night, make the bed,
choose between washing
the windows, the clothes,
the car. Now the coffee's
perked and he carries it
to her in her favorite cup.
She sits up, smiles. He
says he hopes her meeting
goes well. She says she
hopes his day is nice.
The dogs and cats sleep.
He tunes the radio to
the classical station.
She holds the coffee
between her hands.

Laura Cherry

## THE KNOT

I sleep in a groove
hard as pavement
and am beeped awake

in the dark. A knot
in my forehead whispers
*I can't I can't I can't*

through everything
I prove it wrong by doing.
Coffee is my mother now,

speaking gently to the knot
without loosening it.
Some days I have to sing

in the car, joylessly,
just to make it to work alive:
*Hallelujah.*

## MOKARABBIA

È un treno la caffettiera
delle 07.15
in partenza dal primo binario
nella mia cucina
tutte le mattina
festivi compresi
che prendo al volo
fino alla mia stazione
di destinazione
in culo a un sogno
che bevo.
E poi
ritorna indietro.

Francesca Pellegrino
Adria Bernardi (translator)

## MOKAFURY

The 7:15
coffee machine's
a train departing
each morning
track one
from my kitchen
holidays too
which I seize
till my destination station
riding the ass of a dream
that I drink.
Then
the return trip.

## REPEAT UNTIL

Dentro ~~(tra la sveglia e il primo caffè~~
~~sotto la doccia~~
~~nel cassetto che apro~~
~~nella maglia che scelgo~~
~~nel jeans che indosso~~
~~nella chiave che chiude la porta di casa~~
~~nella chiave che mette in moto d'auto~~
~~nel secondo caffè~~
~~nel bagde d'entrata~~
~~nel badge d'uscita~~
~~nel pranzo che se posso volentieri lo salto~~
~~nel terzo caffè~~
~~nel badge di entrata~~
~~nel quarto caffè~~
~~nel badge d'uscita~~
~~nel quinto caffè~~
~~nella chiave che apre la porta di casa~~
~~nella cena che se posso faccio idem col pranzo~~
~~nella maglia e nel jeans che spoglio~~
~~nel pigiama che vesto~~
~~nel sesto caffè)~~ mi cerco
l'amore nelle mani
ma si è fatto buio.

E non ci credo più.

Francesca Pellegrino
Adria Bernardi (translator)

## REPEAT UNTIL

Inside ~~(between waking and the first coffee~~
~~in the shower~~
~~in the drawer I open~~
~~in the sweater I choose~~
~~in the jeans I pull on~~
~~in the key that locks the door of the house~~
~~in the key that starts the car~~
~~in the second coffee~~
~~in the entrance badge~~
~~in the exit badge~~
~~in the lunch that I willingly skip~~
~~in the third coffee~~
~~in the entrance badge~~
~~in the fourth coffee~~
~~in the exit badge~~
~~in the fifth coffee~~
~~in the key that opens the door of the house~~
~~in the dinner I treat the same as lunch~~
~~in the sweater and in the jeans that I take off~~
~~in the pajamas I put on~~
~~in the sixth coffee)~~ I search
love in my hands
but it has gotten dark.

And I no longer believe in it.

## SOMETHING HAS LIFTED

My husband sprints as if
he could outrun his grief—

through the kitchen,
checking his oversized iPhone,

grabbing his keys,
and most days, his wedding ring,

asking, *Did I kiss you yet?*
before shutting the door.

I miss the smell of French Roast
brewing in our house by the beach,

before we got married
and stopped drinking coffee—

our palm tree swaying in wind,
slowly as our days: toasting bagels,

browsing nurseries, planting
flowers in our rented garden,

having sex, napping—
then pressing *repeat.*

Last night, I watched him play
Transformers with Desmond,

for the first time the way
he used to play with Riley,

ending with a dinosaur
on the floor, legs
surrendered to air.
Today, my husband leans easily

against the kitchen counter,
smiling like he used to,

in our bagel days.
Desmond enters, mirroring

his father's smile, their faces
like two halves

of the same broken geode,
as they clean the toys off the floor.

## HOW SHE SERVES YOU

*This being human is a guest house.*
*Every morning a new arrival.*
—Rumi, trans. Coleman Barks

Shame brings you coffee
to wake you. She has laced
it with cinnamon and chicory.
She sits on the edge of your bed,
offers you the warm cup.
This is not what you expected.
For two years, you've kept
the door locked
so she couldn't come in.
Perhaps you thought
she would smell
like rancid sardines.
Perhaps you imagined
she would grasp you
with hideous, deformed
claws and not let you go
or sit on you until you
deflated. Instead,
she is wearing her bathrobe,
as if she's just waking up, too.
She loves you.
She tells you so. She smiles
at you with such sincerity
that there is no way
to not meet her eyes.
Could she be just
another teacher
whose reputation
is worse than her lessons?
She does not bring up
anything you have or have not done.

You do that yourself.
Good Morning, she says.
You choose to believe her.
To your surprise, almost
as if you are watching yourself
and in yourself at the same time,
you hug this unlikely friend.
And then—is it because you
leaned toward her instead
of hiding under the covers again—
she leaves. Just like that.
You almost want her back.
The cup, though bitter,
is easier to drink than
you thought
it would be.
You drink it until
there is nothing left.
God, you feel awake.
As if you could walk
to Wyoming from here.
As if you could rip off
the door lock with your bare hands.
As if you could meet anyone,
even yourself.

## MORNING COFFEE

In my mug the ghost of berries,
cut shine of rubies hand-picked
inside burlap bags rocking on burros
upslope in Columbia, berries grown on trees
speaking the old language of clouds and poverty, seized
each afternoon by the hands of rain,
and shaken like a child from dreams.

It starts here while the toucan sleeps
in rain forest squeezed by ocean and Andes.
Coffee is the eye of Cortez widening to burn herons
and flamingos in Aztec aviaries, coffee
the hand of Quetzalcoatl trembling as he lifts
a smoking mirror to see the blond giant, murdering.

Coffee does not run light as a gecko
across the tongue so much as curl between teeth,
waking me to a neighborhood of sirens
and domestic screams, to the sheetmusic of a mother's laughter
plaiting her daughter's hair, to the insults
of politicians on TV hydroplaning like car tires in a torrent,
to my fingertips drenched in caffeine
tapping like centipedes stampeding my kitchen table
under which the sleeping dog of reason breathes.

Jack Ridl

# OVERCAST IN KEY WEST

The tarpon lie laconic alongside
our little houseboat, their fins slowly

fanning to keep them in place. We
too move in place, letting the boat

welcome the low-knot breeze
as it rocks us, gentle into the gray

day's opening. We have little other
than coffee brewed strong against

the scrim of dispiriting news.
The island's one seaplane slides

onto the ocean's runway as fighter jets
outdistance their roar straight lining

their terrible glide back to base.
The gulls hover, coast, turn, swerve

against, into, and on the updraft, laughing
as they lurk above the open wide bight.

Across my sight, houseboats sit steady
against the pier, each rocking within

the sun's filtered rise, inhabitants here
all but anonymous in their unencumbered

ways of getting by. Soon our dog will open
one eye, yawn, lay his head back down.

Rain is the dogma of the day. We have
our coffee, each other nothing but each other.

## DUTCH FRY BABY

We sit at the island
in my turquoise kitchen
our hands warmed
by hot coffee, by mugs
of stoneware pottery.

When I was young,
you warmed my hands
in the palm of your hands,
or in the pocket
of a Woolrich jacket.

Today's mug up is rooted
in warmth and bribery.
The driveway too slick
to safely maneuver
with shovel is plowed

by you. In turn, the winds
of Ceylon cinnamon blow.
The egg and baked apple,
the butter, flour and brown
sugar counter your bluster.

Like you, this morning
is brisk.

## BIRD

For days now a red-breasted bird
has been trying to break in.
She tests a low branch, violet blossoms
swaying beside her, leaps into the air and flies
straight at my window, beak and breast
held back, claws raking the pane.
Maybe she longs for the tree she sees
reflected in the glass, but I'm only guessing.
I watch until she gives up and swoops off.
I wait for her return, the familiar
click, swoosh, thump of her. I sip cold coffee
and scan the room, trying to see it new,
through the eyes of a bird. Nothing has changed.
Books piled in a corner, coats hooked
over chair backs, paper plates, a cup
half-filled with sour milk.
The children are in school. The man is at work.
I'm alone with dead roses in a jam jar.
What do I have that she could want enough
to risk such failure, again and again?

# I HAD A DREAM

I had a dream last night.
Actually, I had a dream between the alarm clock,
tuned to the jazz station, some kind of bebop,
which Josh forgot to turn off,
which I grumpily stumbled from bed to silence,
and his waking me an hour or so later with coffee and the cat.

I sat up.
I sat up with coffee and the cat.
I drank the coffee, snuggled the cat closer.
I considered writing the dream
but told myself I'd remember it.

I dreamed a dream that declared itself
and now I can't remember it whole,
just a woman with long curly black hair

who resembled my therapist.
This woman who could have been my therapist
led me along a rut that could have been a trench.

I dreamed a dream about a therapist leading me down a trench.
No dream should be that obvious.

But what do I know?
I connect the words to create fragments to create sentences.
Like life, fragments called moments
strung together to create day and night.

Laura Foley

## MY OWN HAND

It's a cappuccino
kind of day,
my way to medicate,
I've come to understand,
my own hand which lifts to me,
as if to say, *Darling*.

# CAST

*Inclinado en las tardes tiro mis tristes redes*
—Pablo Neruda

Everything inside my house is sad today,
the avocado green walls, the scratched plank floors,
even the refrigerator groans.

Outside the trees are sad:
the maple stooped over the neighbor's chain-link fence,
the cedars' wide branches weeping into the lawn.

A tall man at the bus stop, asking change for a dollar,
waving the bill at half-mast, is sad.

At the Safeway, a perky blonde cashier suppresses tears,
stacking the onions atop the bread
in the sad paper sack.

Then all the cars in the street are sad,
foreign, domestic, all coming sadly
to a stop at the same dejected stop sign.

And the streets themselves are sad,
wearing numbers like inmate I.D.'s.

When I get back home, sunshine
is flowing from the skylight into the kitchen
like a sad yellow rain over the chopping-block island.

Dust motes are dancing in it—Flamenco-style—
sadness be damned!

I make a tuna sandwich with sliced onions,
my tears drip into a fresh brewed cup of coffee.
Lunch is good—even the refrigerator purrs.

Jeanne Bryner

## THE BREAD OF LONGING

Let us enter under a blistered white lintel,
moving slowly, heavily, our arms interlaced.
Let the foyer mirror be ordinary,
your gray bathrobe, my mended flannel gown.
Let our pockets be filled with the paper money
of quiet mornings. Let us have one knife
and the strength to slice the bread of longing
on the kitchen counter. Let the table with its pale blue
chairs be bathed in sunlight for the old card game
of small talk, the simple fog of tea, the coffee's
darkness. Let us speak in syllables of settled debts,
survival and unfrenzied corridors. Let our words
taste textured as aged cheddar. Let us unravel the silk
colors of knowledge, a smooth language folded,
saved by protective paper. Let us gaze in wonder
and surprise at the violet's fixed position of purple
and the wind's sassy motion forcing gingham curtains apart.
Let us have a pencil and a bottle for this note.
Let us smile at the marked calendar of our best days.

# iii.

# Literary Latte

*I have measured out my life with coffee spoons;*

—T.S. Eliot

Alicia Ostriker

# WAITING FOR THE LIGHT

*for Frank O'Hara*

Frank, we have become an urban species
   at this moment many millions of humans are
      standing on some corner waiting like me

for a signal permitting us to go,
   a signal depicting a small pale pedestrian
      to be followed by a sea-green light

we do not use this opportunity
   to tune in to eternity
      we bounce upon our toes impatiently

It is a Thursday morning, Frank, and I feel
   rather acutely alive but I need a thing of beauty
      or a theory of beauty to reconcile me

to the lumps of garbage I cannot love enclosed
   in these tough shiny black plastic bags
      heaped along the curb of 97th Street, my street—

like a hideous reminder of the fate we all expect
   letting the bulky slimy truth of waste
      attack our aesthetic sense and joie de vivre

reliably every Thursday. Let me scan the handsome amber
   columned and corniced dwellings
      reflected in rear windows of parked cars, let me wish

luck to their hives of intimacies, people
   in kitchens finishing a morning coffee
      saying see you later to the ones they live with

Let me raise my eyes to the blue veil adrift
    between and above the artifice of buildings
        and at last I am slipping through a flaw in time

where the string of white headlights approaching, the string
    of red taillights departing, seem as if
        they carry some kind of message

perhaps the message is that one block west
    Riverside Park extends its length
        at the edge of Manhattan like the downy arm

of a tender, amusing, beautiful lover,
    and after that is the deathless river
        but waiting for the light feels like forever

Over a cup of coffee or sitting on a park bench or walking the dog, he would recall some incident from his youth—nothing significant—climbing a tree in his backyard, waiting in left field for a batter's swing, sitting in a parked car with a girl whose face he no longer remembered, his hand on her breast and his body electric; memories to look at with curiosity, the harmless behavior of a stranger, with nothing to regret or elicit particular joy. And although he had no sense of being on a journey, such memories made him realize how far he had traveled, which, in turn, made him ask how he would look back on the person he was now, this person who seemed so substantial. These images, it was like looking at a book of old photographs, recognizing a forehead, the narrow chin, and perhaps recalling the story of an older second cousin, how he had left long ago to try his luck in Argentina or Australia. And he saw that he was becoming like such a person, that the day might arrive when he would look back on his present self as on a distant relative who had drifted off into uncharted lands.

## ON PICKING UP THE PENNY

At risk of contracting a microbial virulence
I picked up the penny, after which I stepped
on a sidewalk's crack under a ladder while
a black cat scampered across my trajectory
to Dunkin Donuts, where for the 387th day
in a row I'd spent $3.37 on an outsized cup
of iced joe and neglected to tip upon leaving
the pleasant enough homeless gentleman
that holds the door open for each and every
soul that enters and exits the purgatorial
franchise, my logic being the usual mélange
of self-aggrandizement and school of hard
knocks condescension that rationalizes my
otherwise left-leaning position on handouts,
so today I figured what the hell I'd bestow
upon him this coppery, fortuitous artifact
but he affably declined, citing his recent
move to only accept payment via Apple Pay.

Dale Jensen

## FAST AS A NEW YORK SONNET

down this horizonless sidewalk of coffee
the buildings are supported by the doors of coffeehouses
the sidewalk runs as fast as caffeine will carry it
each step each stride each dance step its very own

some day     some say
the free music will end and you'll have to pay the piper
for all the shoe soles you've worn out on these walks
but you'll only have to teach the piper a new tune

noah's ark landed in washington square park
it landed there over and over again
at least every five or ten years it landed
but lots of times it rains and washes the old footprints away
people forget about that even with coffee
that's why this place is so wonderful

Marian Kaplun Shapiro

# WAITING

becomes an exercise in empty-
ness like the coffee mug
before the water boils, your taste
buds tingling, your nostrils wanting sensing
something in the air, the not yet
not yet putt putt perking, popping
its caffeinated castanets faster faster
filling you with hope dread wish excitement dis-
appointment maybe when if how the thunder be-
fore the lightning the time after the wing flaps open
        and the airplane lands
(at last) the waiting waiting for the moment *when* when
the waiting *is* becomes the waiting *was*, the when itself,
the when it is not, and when
is it not?

Jeffrey Johannes

## SILENCE

Sometimes fog
surrounds morning
in a white room;
then the silence
of sunlight seeps
into balsam shadows.
Steam is silence too,
slipping over the brim
of bone china
in the coffee-quiet
of morning.

Diane Henningfeld

## DO NOT GO MUZZY

*after Dylan Thomas*

Do not go muzzy into morning light,
Your eyes should open at the start of day;
Brew, brew at dawn, the ending of the night.

Wise women waken, know they must be bright,
and drink a mocha or a latte. They
Do not go muzzy into morning light.

Good women see their childhood dreams take flight,
Learn to do what needs the doing, and always
Brew, brew at dawn, the ending of the night.

Wild women drink their joe with gin and fight
Their demons, stomp and walk right in—they
Do not go muzzy into morning light.

Grave women want their coffee black and right
away. "Alexa, start the pot," they say,
"Brew, brew, at dawn, the ending of the night."

And you, my coffee, help my words take flight.
Bless me, give me strength to face the day.
I will not go muzzy into morning light.
I've brewed at dawn, the ending of the night.

sliver of a moon
between my teeth
coffee sugar

## COFFEE

Cut the vein in this wrist.
And thick black liquid will bubble out.
Matters little if I have five cups
or no coffee at all,
hands shake just the same,
body jitters to some invisible music.
Eyes half open, or half close.
The world is still a blur.
The left turns so far left
that they take on the mantle of the right.
I'm afraid to send out this poem.
Seventeen high school students were killed
on Valentine's Day this year.
I haven't slept in a thousand years,
and I'm only 45.
A year ago, the president signed a bill
making it easier for those suffering
from mental illness to buy guns.
My wife is donating the money
I made from a poetry reading
to a group demanding gun control.
Our baby daughter wakes me up
with her crying.
I hold her to my chest.
My hand is rubbing her back.
Outside, the night is completely black.
No stars in sight.

Jeffrey Johannes

## VISITATION
*for Monet*

He strolls through
my second cup
of coffee,
a cathedral seeking
sunlight and hay;
his cravat a brushstroke,
paint splattered,
accents his beard.
He gavottes
across blue tile,
a water lily dancing
toward my sunroom door.

Emily Shearer

## WOLVES, GUESTS

You were adamant that I invite the wolves in
to dine and when they came to the door,
I did not let them

cross the threshold. You bore in your body
the music of stolen poetics:
the warp and weft, the heft of pen, the tense thread

and the spinning wheel; you formed of me
a bird and filled my hollow bones
with fallow flight.

You built of me a bright breezeway of arches
you needed to cross through to freely move
from lone wolf to wanted guest,

from black coffee, strong tea
to honey, cream and sugar,
from a locked stash of red apples    to pomegranates

smashed open for the taking, from the pause of a sentence
to the lyric of a song, the vivace of a cyclone, adagio of slow Sundays
and sweet pie and the paddle of my rowboat

lapping up the ripples; the wolves, lapping up the cream.

# END OF MANKIND

The taps will still drip
even as the oceans sweep away.
Turbulent time
will leave the hours, the minutes,
sore and bleeding in some alleyway
but rusted clocks will tick on,
will measure the absence
of coughs and spit,
of crazy laughter and stupid tears.
As new mountains are thrust up by the core
radios will continue to play.
In an unruly mix of hydrogen and oxygen,
old cigarette butts will smolder
for years, no matter what the gas.
Every flash and explosion
and gut-wrench
of raw and rolling geology
will attempt to obliterate,
begin again,
but even without a living soul,
mankind won't let go the traces.
I sit by the window,
sip coffee, look out at a violent world.
My life's in mortal danger.
Only the sip is safe.

# AS CLOSE TO FEELING HUMAN
# AS IT GETS

*"It's hard to argue that we aren't living in a simulated world."*
—Neil deGrasse Tyson (2017)

My familiar mug, I choose to think, is real
enough; brown stains inside don't seem to change
in color much, or disappear. Outside,
the Monty Python Killer Rabbit cartoon
printed on ceramic looks similar
to yesterday's, unless my perceptions
are edited—implanted by a handler,
some teenage punk who holds the game controller

in a universe above my own. Sprawled
on a ratty couch in Momma's basement,
he could tap my favored vessel off the map,
forcing me to sip from flowered china,
or a too-hot Buckstars cardboard cup,
or a caffeinated river,
he could twist warm liquid molecules
into sarin gas, or slide them straight to urine.

Key tap: coffee beans are dug from mines
in Madagascar. Key tap: civil war begins.
Key tap: drones destroy all coffee mines.

My mug's interior flashes into bone-dry
white. Worldwide coffee shortages ensue,
creating Holland Tulip Panic prices
in a George Miller directed world:
where I'm shrunk into a boring orc,
where gasoline has been replaced
by Folgers Crystals, where I remain
the identical junkie in each universe.

Robert M. Randolph

## CUP OF BLUES

My first cup of morning coffee
tastes like delta blues. Down in the Maxwell House
somebody's using a bottleneck for a slide,
playing a vintage Gibson.

At first I thought it was Robert Johnson
playing a 1926 L-1,
but it's Furry Lewis on his B-25-N.
I heard him in an auditorium years ago,
and his music has made its way into this brew.

At one point, back then,
he chorded with his elbow; that's in there too,
along with my drive home that night
after the gig, with my now ex-wife.

She and I talked our blues.
Now, some forty years later, Furry is playing
in E tuning in this morning's coffee,
so I'll get my A key Hohner Marine Band harmonica
and play cross harp.

# THE MATERIAL VS. THE SPIRITUAL

On the day when four men carry all the taped boxes,
the chairs and tables, the knickknacks down
the steep driveway, pack two trucks and pilot them
through narrow streets to hoist and carry
each object into another house
and stack them in the empty corresponding rooms,
on the day I scurry from one house
to the other, driving my mother's coffee table
to the storage locker with Larry's mother's china,
directing the movers as their shouts
echo up stairwells, down hallways,
while my knees ache and my feet swell,
on the day when there's no hot water and I
can't find the cups, a day when we decide
what to do with each half-full bottle,
the bent trowel, the button
that vaguely reminds me of something that's been
missing it, several hundred scraps of paper
marked by my hand, a stray mothball or two,
it's hard to believe in a life that exists
apart from this one, a transcendent glimmer
as elusive as the slit in the skinny shaft
of the needle, the needle itself buried
in a box whose label I can't decipher,
can't even think about
until I've found, somewhere,
the coffee.

## LUKEWARM

We all have them: days as bland as
coffee forgotten on the counter.
Times when there's nothing *special* to say;
no one's getting married, no one's dying.

Muddy days when the world blurs into beige,
neither the black of French Roast
nor the white of milk.

A blend you pour down the sink
because it's not what you wanted—
or swallow, resigned to tepid

though there's always a chance
you might peer inside, see something new
like a swirl of light on the surface of your drink
and begin to wonder
if even coffee grown cold can comfort;
if it's only bland because you've known better.
A sip, another, and you taste what's there:
a trace of sugar, a hint of warmth.
The choice to reheat what once was hot.

James Rodgers

Four o' clock dead zone:
too late for coffee, but too
soon for tequila

Ilona Hegedus

# END-OF-YEAR COFFEE POEM

Perfect for a date or for meeting old acquaintances,
it might be one of your longest relationships.
A life-long friend.
A coffee is there when you make new friends,
when you lose some friends and when you fall in love.
You get addicted when you're still young, and the admiration
is a lasting one. It's still there when your hair turns grey.
Summer sun, autumn leaves, winter cold or springtime and joy.
Sadness, sleepiness or just existing.
Anything can be an occasion for a cup.
Before work, before Christmas shopping, or before classes...
You can always count on coffee.

## PLACE

Computer eyestrain headaches, paper cuts,
Cramped lower back, and carpal tunnel throb.
My desk: a stack of stacks and paper cups
Of paper clips or cold beige coffee. Job:
I need your tasks. You keep me off the skids
Of alcoholic alleyways, their brick
Cliff sky and puddles. You supply my kids
And pay my bills. Sometimes you make me sick
Of life, yet ruts provide some comfort, grooves
I needn't plow anew each week. My chums
Commiserate and cheer. There's lakes and groves
Each month on calendar. There's tea and Tums
For tension, projects focusing each sprawling day,
My office window over sunny silver bay.

M. J. Iuppa

## COFFEE (BREAK)

Minding   my own cup   they talk

heads cocked      looking down

into a deep stain      on the tablecloth

A cryptic pause      hush
& buzz   the pot back
on the burner

Their eyes   stretch   hello

into good bye

without saying a word

The gurgle of whispers
trail behind me   foamy
dismissal
other business

implores   more talk   inches away

delicious bits

sputter of laughter

two   who know      plenty

Heidi Seaborn

## A WRITER'S WINTER

Husked afternoon—
I scavenge words
from what I pick

out of my teeth,
the slight taste
of cardamom. Tongue

hot with coffee
and bourbon, a life lived
on the sharp end of a knife.

# HOW TO DISAPPEAR

*after Marjorie Stelmach,*
*"How to Disappear without a Trace"*
*packing up my studio after a residency*

Close up your books,
they're only leaves from dead trees.
Suck the ink back into your pen.
Shut your notebook; it's only
the record of a past which is already
slipping away. Put the lid on your laptop,
its random bits and bytes. Disconnect
the internet, email, Facebook; nobody's
going to miss you when you're gone.
Pack up: paper clips, post-its, pencils.
And your mug—coffee, the true ink
that fuels the writer's pen. Close the door,
turn out the light. All the unwritten words
will come to life, party in the exhaled air,
like dust motes dancing in the slanted sun.

David D. Horowitz

# FRIDAY EVENING'S FIFTY STORIES

The stapler's whapped its final document
In this fluorescent week. No conference calls
Till buzzing Monday. Drop a chocolate mint
In mug of decaf blend, and stir. The walls
Remain as beige as patience. Exit signs
Burn emerald stencil through the shadowed halls
As fifty stories down a siren whines
Some faint emergency, and tension falls
From tired heart. Oh, what a week—a waltz
Across a minefield, stroll through shooting range.
The scarlet rose I bought last Monday wilts,
But twilight—opal after Thursday's rains.

# TOO MANY REASONS NOT
# TO GO HOME

Because the hum of an endless road entices.

You're just another nameless traveler
in the juggernaut at any gas station hub.

Because you'd rather pine for those chased by wildfire
    in one country,
than to heart-harden over the presidential tweets of another.

Mountains enjoy a morning serenade of hot coffee
and propped-up legs,
easy chatter of the moment, play.

The sky will close its vast blue eye
and suddenly, again, your world
shrouds in mist grays and green.

Should you choose to not return, send
for the daughter's cat. She misses him terribly.

coffee
life breath
matter of honor
battle denial
death

Joshua Gage

## ODE TO COFFEE

I curl into this corner booth
and cradle your black fire.
Your obsidian blade
cuts through limp pancakes
and greasy hash browns.
Some men would have you
adorned with a negligee
of milk froth or glittered
with diamonds of sugar,
but I want nothing more
than your cherry perfume
and bitter kisses. Now,
in the hour when life
becomes a tomb, warm me
with your canticle of the earth.

Patrick Donnelly

## INSTANT COFFEE

When every winged thing
was falling for sweetness
        in my cup,
in the last dregs of light
at the end of a sunset dock,
        I gave up
and poured it in the lake,
and watched that cloud of cream
        expand and hold
an instant in the dark water,
before summer knelt
        into the cold,
dispersing her bright crystals.

## MUG SHOT

Lashed to a sugar cube, looking for coffee in my mug, I have on my anti-scald wet suit and teaspoon-shaped flippers and gloves. It is pure desire that reduced and placed me on this cube in the first place. When nose and tongue await flavor, it is best that such desire precede the actual occasion of sips. I know to tie myself down, so as not to be jostled and fall off when the cube is dropped.

Every day starts somewhere between geometry and water. I plop into my mug and start stirring swimming. I also add my ego into the mug, let it dissolve, and I sip slowly. There is always a hot way to swallow pride. It is a lot like gulping flippers, gloves, and all.

Scientists say that after liquid is stirred in a vessel at least one molecule returns to its original position once the liquid settles. What about being emotionally 'stirred'? What position does one return to?

As caffeine begins to whirl my nervous system, I sense it as a pinwheel spinning in morning fog, that same fog that lifted off the pillow with me.

Every scintilla of morning is on a need to row basis: gravity and hustle will split their boats. What to do and how to do all and everything? Behind every door, answers eavesdrop on the deft noise of questions. To sip, perchance to dream....

## MUSE

My muse is no god. I'm not sure
he even believes in God. He tells me
fishing is his church. And I believe him.

Every fifth or sixth Sunday, he wakes
early, in need of some religion.
He pulls his poles and tackle box

from the shed, eases his truck
down our street, leaves me
a little coffee in the pot.

All day, he worships
in his granddad's boat,
on his parents' pond.

He catches little,
but releases
everything.

## HOW TO FIND GEORGE STERLING:
## REVISE THE CANON

At first, you should do nothing more daring than go
to the Castro and sip a double espresso at the Cafe Flore.
Enough caffeine? Then slide into North Beach,
solidify in an opium den. You'll find George Sterling
seated, sharing a water pipe with Robinson Jeffers.
Be sure to save enough coffee so you can hike up
Telegraph Hill, walk on wooden boards to the shanties
that brought Kerouac such joy. Push right on through
commuters waiting for the bus under big gold letters
of City Lights Bookstore with doors that protect pyramids
of *On the Road* and Ginsberg's *Howl*. You won't find
Sterling's *Lilith* or *Testimony of the Suns*. Grab a latte.
at Starbucks. Let fog digest you. To find George Sterling,
you must secret yourself on top of Russian Hill. When
it is one half hour before sunset, go to the end of a path.
You will know the one; it is overgrown. What you will
find is rather small, a stone cut in the only words
by Sterling left in San Francisco that you can finger:

*Tho the dark be cold and blind, / Yet her sea-fog's touch*
*is kind, / And her mightier caress / Is joy and the pain*
*thereof; / And great is thy tenderness, / O cool, grey city of love!*

## LO, YON CUP RUNNETH

Shakespeare's curses crisscross my coffee cup,
a jarring jollop to jumpstart the day.

*Light of brain*, get your butt up. *Highly-fed
and lowly taught*, the words won't stir themselves.

No artificial sweeteners here. Perhaps
to bed. The nuns spoke true, unholy miss,

*lewdly inclin'd*. Oh, bawdy Bard, did not
you ever stray from toil? *You scullion*,

work 'til you are *roast-meat for worms*. Oh, Will,
*infinite and endless liar*, whence your

dark lady and sweet boy? *O Gull, O dolt,
as ignorant as dirt*, believing all

you find in gleeking books. Out, out, Damned Cup,
*I do desire we be better strangers.*

# KAHVEH

*(Kahveh: the Ottoman Turkish word for coffee)*

Let me remind you, brothers and sisters
that in the beginning there was fruit
and the heart of the fruit was baptised in the fire
because all men love darkness
and the bitter pit shone in all its glory.
Praise be to the fire!

And I want to tell you people
and there are many who don't understand
that the almighty savour is divine
blessed succour in your hour of need
and you shall know him as Kahveh.
Praise be to the savour!

And I say to you now, I am a sinner
but believe me when I tell you
that in the morning there will be light
and in the evening—dark.
Sisters and brothers, fear not the trembling in your heart
let your eyes be opened
Praise be to the light and dark!

Brothers and sisters, hear my words
scorn the idle worshipers who cast their spoon in the jar
pity the weak who are not blessed by the pestle of his power
pity them for they know not the torrefaction of his passion.
I say to you now—swallow him!
Swallow him all the days of your life.

Let me ask you again, people
is he not the seed of our salvation?
Praise him, for he is good
serve him with gladness and chocolate

baclava, iced bun and jammy toast
anoint him with a cherished spirit
Praised be the angelic host!
Praise be to Kahveh!

Su Shafer

## ODE TO THE DARK OVERLORD OF MY SOUL

Elixir of life,
The liquid essence of Fortitude.
Encouragement's honey gold
Slow roasted to Resilience's bold and bitter burnt.
But oh! The mellifluous hope glowing from
Its umber depths, visible
In the arcing pour and musical swirl
As my cup is filled.
It hits my nose like a warm promise
And my palate like a jolt of concentrated temerity.
My pluck is awakened.
I can take this day.

# THE BARISTA ASKS HOW I
# LIKE MY COFFEE

Belligerent and beckoning as an unanswered
text, something between a death
threat and a booty call.

Beans slow-roasted under a fire
blinding as klieg lights,
a police interrogation.

Pulverize them to pencil shavings, think
the hooves of Iberian bulls caged
in a Spanish galleon's bilge.

Next, make a brass kettle moan an old spiritual:
Baptize the beans in its scalding waters—
dark as the Mississippi Delta.

Plunge the brew in a press-pot the size of a giant's syringe,
then decant into a mug the marble of tombstone.
Watch its steam ghost into

a question mark as you peer into its depths,
still as a Nietzschean abyss,
a dead God in its sediment dregs.

Into this round pitch, pour the white from a blank page
until it gyres into a golden ratio, a milky nebula,
my hale, bitter beginning.

# A SYNDICATE OF BARISTAS

follows orders issued by the bossa
nova—he of the killer smile,

tuxedoed feet. *Death by caffeine*, he spits,
lethal intentions frothing at his mouth,

his facial espresso a blend
of sin and cinnamon. Oh, time,

you know it's up when Big Joe
denies you mocha, offers

a jolt of cyanide you can't refuse
beneath a dollop of tainted whipped cream.

No chance for a confession, your funeral
music already a samba recessional.

Pity the latte departed,
betrayed by pumpkin spice. Once

you keel over they will bury you
with your ceramic mug. Some thug

spent all night digging a space
your size in coffee-colored ground.

Elizabeth Aoki

# EIGHT WAYS OF LOOKING AT A LATTE
*(with apologies to Wallace Stevens' blackbirds)*

I grasp, protected through my long sleeves, and still love burns
like I'm holding a latte.

This latte seems solid, but the bottom of the cup has as arch,
like a dancer's foot. A mind could be safe in there, out of the rain.

Thoughts circle around and around this topic like the writing
on cups of paper and Styrofoam.

Tropical night, in a Victorian hotel room filled with lace two
brown bodies strive for the hot foam of sex.
They steam. We steam with them.

I am speeding like night across the continent of Africa. My hair
is caught in final ochre of sunset as the Land Rover heads for
the safety of the city lights. My white hat is a lid that says solo
traveler. I am a latte.

All the people I speak with today blur in speech.
Their hands wave in the air without ceasing: *jabber, jabber,jabber.*
They do not know how to hold still. They pour over.

We wonder what it means to be conscious, *bing!*
What if our silicon sisters, our machines, will be
able to replicate this feat of self-refraction, requiring
the caffeine jolt to wake, liquid keys in the ignition?

Like spiral arms of carbon and the centers of stars, like
the passing of a tree into full autumn blaze and hearth,
all this
swirling in an old slipper bathtub—my life, your life—
is now our latte, cold too soon.

## STOPPING BY STARBUCKS ON A SNOWY EVENING

*with apologies to Robert Frost*

Whose beans these are I think I know.
They're ground to brew and packed to go.
No one will see me stopping here
To warm my gut with mugs of Joe.

The head barista's feeling queer
From many shots of black liqueur.
She's had much more than she can take
Of serving scones and coffee cake.

She gives her mocha hair a shake
To tell me there is no mistake.
The only other sound's the sweep
Of credit cards and change she makes.

Her latte's lovely, dark and deep,
But I have lines to rhyme, then break,
And miles to go before I wake,
And miles to go before I wake.

## SERVING SUGGESTIONS

Apply a cubist grid to that French
cruller hovering near the mirror
of your mouth, square by square
release the sum of its sweet tonalities
until the oasis of its middle will reveal
a theorem you may find sublime.

As day progresses your neurons
should be busy consuming choline,
so any donut display case will do.
Rhyme, yet don't over rhyme
those zones of fillings, twists,
and frostings, disclaimers always
part of the package, but a Long John
Custard and black coffee in a diner
could save your mind.

## BLACK COFFEE

Let no vague shapes milk
Into this darkness as at dawn.
The east blossoms clumsily with light.

Let nothing disturb
The bitter grounds
That dispute beyond words.

Pour blackness before me:
Let it ink the white
China like slugs of lead
Garrulous as a cityroom
Putting the news to bed.

I will drink it strong,
Unsweetened. It is not taste
That lures my tongue
But the impulse to waken

On nerve's edge
Like a black brew
Percolating over a flame
In the witch-hour when
My own face alarms me.

## STORY FOR A DULL WORLD

Those coffee-drinking monks knew what they were doing.
I can see them now in their cappuccino-colored robes,
running to morning prayers, planting rutabagas with zeal,
illuminating manuscripts in flagrant teal and wild vermilion.

Those monks had pizzazz. Their eighteen-hour days
passed in the wink of a dilated pupil. They were supermonks,
their devotion unprecedented, their energy infinite,
their coffee plantations fingering the horizon.

One year the crop failed. Leaves slowly browned,
turned papery as tobacco. When the last plant was lost
the monks mourned, chanting feverishly. A few
martyred themselves. Then the headaches struck. None
        survived.

## MOURNING COFFEE

Where is that thought
so searing with insight
that it burns a hole in the paper?
That causes some smoke alarm
to go off somewhere
in this place in which we live?

Where are the words
so exacting to describe it?
That start out so hot to the touch
                then simmer
          then cool
then get crumpled and tossed
into some recycling bin?
That is if lucky enough to have reached
the nirvana of hard copy—
that ancient proof of existence.

Has anyone actually ever witnessed
something in the process of getting recycled?
                We take it on faith

that the tan coffee filter
through which I'm about to let water flow
has been here before.
A journey in Hinduism
that keeps coming back in one form or another
'til it gets it right?
            But I live but once

compelled to go on in search of words
I never had in mind
to describe a mind for which there are no words.
Perhaps I should take to finger paints

to attempt what to make of this cup of time?
Let clocks drip as Dali did?
Or simply sit and smell the coffee
having run out of free verse
or reason to rhyme.

# iv.

# Elegy with Coffee

*Coffee smells like freshly ground heaven.*

—Terri Guillemets

Margo Berdeshevsky

## WINTER WE DO NOT KNOW

Winter, we don't know how long a tree
wants to live   How long there is—to see

Winter, black inks of morning    her
burned thought like twice warmed coffee

in hand    we are so much stiller than we
used to be—deaths of dream in sleep-burnt

cups in hand    We know there is    now and
later    Winter, do you think everyone is afraid

of a body?
*Star light, star bright*—give me help me

*bless me let me  —*  Break my thin lipped skeleton
wide tonight    find a holy hand in it    waiting

A hot promise:    *You're ok, darling*    A word
sacred as a torn skin before the fall    A breath

before we forget    Sacred as a friend's begging bowl
Our plate of wisdom — raw —

You who can fathom a hand to wake us more gently
stroke us through this

too ancient and too new air    would it be still
reverent after our long winter—to touch what is gray?

To open a curtain, to slake the morning's thirst?
Swallow what is warm, and kind — in memory, say —

[*I came to explore the wreck—Adrienne Rich*]

145

## PRECIOSA LIKE A LAST CUP OF COFFEE

*for my grandmother, Luisa Roig, 1908-1997*
*Carolina, Puerto Rico*

Tata says her wheelchair
has been stolen by the nurses.
She hallucinates the ceiling fan
spinning closer, the vertigo
of a plummeting helicopter,
but cannot raise her hands
against the blades. Her legs jerk
with the lightning that splits trees.
She scolds her dead sister,
who studies Tata's face
from a rocking chair by the bed
but does not answer.
The grandchildren are grateful
for the plastic diaper, the absence of bedsores.

Tata's mouth collapses without teeth;
her words are miners blackened in the hole.
Now a word pushes out: *café*.
*No coffee for her, or she won't eat,*
says the nurse.

Tata craves more than a puddle
in a styrofoam cup:
the coffee farm in Utuado, 1928,
the mountains hoisting a harvest of clouds,
the beans a handful of planets,
the spoon in the cup a silver oar,
and the roosters' bickering choir.

But no coffee today.
Cousin Bernice crawls into the bed,
stretches her body across Tata's body

146

like a drowsy lover, mouth hovering
before her grandmother's eyes
as she chants the word: *Preciosa.*

*Preciosa* like the song,
chorus brimming from a kitchen radio
on West 98th Street after the war,
splashing down the fire escape,
*preciosa te llaman:*
an island from the sky
or a last cup of coffee.
Tata repeats: *Preciosa.*

The song bathes her tongue.

## MOTHER'S COFFEE

She made it every day. Drip by drip it trickled
from the filter into the clear glass pot, weak

and with little taste, the 5FU, the leukovorin
still in her veins from yesterday's chemo.

She would pour my cup first, line up
her giant horse pills, CPT-11, Toumadex

on the saucer, then place them on the back
of her throat swallowing hard, almost gagging

with each sip. At the table I pulled out the classified
section from *The New Times* circling teaching jobs

in Connecticut. After gulping down another pill,
she asked, *Why do you want to move to Connecticut?*

*Can't Jim get a job on Long Island? You know I don't
drive over bridges.* I said, *You can visit on weekends.*

She shoves her last pill down, swallows hard, says,
*Your brothers should take the cars, Anthony, the Volvo,*

*Joe the Cadillac. You, you should take the furniture.
You will be the first to have a house, a family.* I push

my coffee aside, shout, *You are not dead yet.*
*Soon,* she says. And when she is done giving

away the furniture and the car, she shuffles
over to the coffee, lifts the pot, asks, *More?*

# STOOP-SITTING WITH DADDY

*Qué hambre*
*de saber*
*cuántas*
*estrellas tiene el cielo!*
—Pablo Neruda

Late one moonless night,
I sneak onto the brick front stoop
of the house where I grew up
and sit, pulling my knees
close to my chest to muffle
the clamor of my clanging heart.

The new owners have not tended
the home, nor the yew bushes
Daddy clipped into goblet shapes,
hours of back-straining labor.
The grass is mostly crab now,
with a battalion of dandelions
that never infiltrated
on my father's watch.

It's late August, a cricket-less
calm settled over the sticky,
mosquito-studded air,
and the sky overhead full
of constellations.

I am reminded of those endless
summer nights,
when doused in bug spray,
Daddy and I used to count
the stars out loud,
a father-daughter song
with no lyrics but numbers.

Daddy was Orion, the bull-slayer,
brave hero, and I was
his little bear,
ready to slake his thirst
by running inside
to put on the kettle,
pour a cup of Sanka,
hot, black.

And my tongue almost tastes
our favorite ice cream,
Breyers' mint chip,
always only one
aqua Melamine dish
for our two-spoon,
stoop-sitting happiness.

Daddy pointed out constellations too,
until my eyes blurred from squinting
to make the patterns match their names,
until my sleepy-headedness
made the sky seem filled with nothing
but bright, luminous sheep.

Right now, a shooting star
ghosts across the sky,
and in my mind,
the screen door squeaks open—
Daddy arriving to sit beside me
on the stoop to count,
one last time.

## STALE COFFEE

I used to make fun of my dad for reheating
leftover coffee to drink in the afternoon.

Now I find myself doing it; his voice
ringing in my head:
*Still good… nothing wrong with it…*
*tastes the same… shame to*
*waste it.*

Post-mortem, his Depression-era logic
convinces me; maybe my standards
are slipping as time conflates?

Tomorrow morning I won't remember
what afternoon coffee tasted like
but I'll still savor the way a man with
a moral compass once made the
world feel safe.

# COFFEE IN THE AFTERNOON

It was afternoon tea, with tea foods spread out
Like in the books, except that it was coffee.

She made a tin pot of cowboy coffee, from memory,
That's what we used to call it, she said, cowboy coffee.

The grounds she pinched up in her hands, not a spoon,
And the fire on the stove she made from a match.

I sat with her and talked, but the talk was like the tea food,
A little of this and something from the other plate as well,

Always with a napkin and a thank-you. We sat and visited
And I watched her smoke cigarettes

Until the afternoon light was funny in the room,
And then we said our good-byes. The visit was liniment,

The way the tea was coffee, a confusion plain and nice,
A balm for the nerves of two people living in the world,

A balm in the tenor of its language, which spoke through
    our hands
In the small lifting of our cups and our cakes to our lips.

It was simplicity, and held only what it needed.
It was a gentle visit, and I did not see her again.

Ellen Bass

# POEM WRITTEN IN THE SIXTH
# MONTH OF MY WIFE'S ILLNESS

I didn't know that when my mother died, her grave
would be dug in my body. And when I weaken,
she is here, dressing behind the closet door,
hooking up her long-line cotton bra,
then sliding the cups around to the front,
leaning over and harnessing each heavy breast,
setting the straps in the grooves on her shoulders,
reins for the journey. She's slicking her lips with
Fire and Ice. She's shoveling the car out of the snow.
How many pints of Four Roses did she slide
into exactly-sized brown bags? How many cases
of Pabst Blue Ribbon did she sling onto the counter?
All the crumpled bills, steeped in the smells
of the lives who'd handled them—their sweat,
their body heat, cheap cologne, onions and
grease, lumber and bleach—she opened
her palm and smoothed each one. Then
stacked them up precisely, restoring order.
And at ten, after the change fund was counted,
the doors locked, she uncinched the girth, unbuckled
the bridle. Cooked Cream of Wheat for my father,
mixed a milkshake with Hershey's syrup for me,
and poured herself a single highball,
placed on a pink or yellow paper napkin.
But this morning I think of a scene I never
witnessed, though she told me the story years later.
She'd left my father in the hospital—this time
they didn't know if he'd pull through—
and driving the hour back to the store, stopped
in a diner and ordered coffee.
She sat in the booth, silently crying
and sipping the hot black coffee,
and the waitress, she told me, never said a word,
just kept refilling her cup.

# BLUE COLLAR ELEGY

*in memoriam Raymond Waters*
*1925-1993*

Not for him this romantic
  burgeoning of distant leafsmoke
    that fringes southern bayberry,
  nor any of the thousand rills
fingering wild rice this dead man's dawn in the sanctuary.

He's nowhere among sweet seepage,
  nor greening the parasitic
    mistletoe, the edible pokeweed,
  the trumpet creeper, nor can I find him
restless in the rectangular bark of the persimmon.

He worked and, when not working,
  *worked*, so now must inhabit
    catwalks and ancient plumbing,
  good citizen of the underworld,
pleased to hear such familiar knocking, the ceaseless

rumble from pipes needing to be wrenched
  apart, realigned, soldered,
    the labyrinthine works below
  New York City ready to shake loose
unless someone labors along with his box of drill bits,

his knuckled rows of sockets,
  flashlight clipped to his belt,
    whistling a solo
  by Dizzy Gillespie, swinging
from one curved forefinger his thermos of black coffee.

Debra Andrea Ahrens

# BLEEDING SCAR

a plain day (*Friday*)
coffee (*black*)
with a friend (*a diner*)

suddenly (*sharp breath*)
crushing pain (*grip mug*)
contract my focus (*small spill*)
to stifle the scream (*lips tight*)

strangled heart (*the empty mug*)
and this thought (*shoes untied*)
that you will never (*cold sheets*)
return home again (*one key*)

but how to
explain fresh
blood from an
ancient wound?

# MIDNIGHT CALL

Our stop and go advance
toward the rolled over van is
wordless.  Breathless.   Until

we see them climb
from the upended doors,
one by one, dazed but
smiling. Happy,
(if happiness travels
this close to death)
for their wobbly legs,
their hungry lungs.
The wind's snowy persistence.

And seeing the survivors' array
of ski hats and bright mittens rising
into the storm's white advance,
we reach for our coffee.
We breathe. We are gone.

Not that all walk away.
My brother, for one.
Shifting
to the opposing lane
just as the oncoming car
crossed the line.

The moment they both
caught their mistake.
Their attempt to return...

Not that I know
that night.  That road.

I barely know (as one
might know
a hard-earned truth)
the call that, strangely,
came to me.  His sister.  Only

his sister. Who knows
how the call skirted
his wife? Skirted our mother.

His boys, now, are grown.
They don't know I got that call.
But when I see them, I hear
the phone ring. I turn
to the wall and try
to return to sleep.

In the only dream
to which I cling
past bed, past
morning,
my sons and
my brother's sons
emerge from doors
dazed and smiling.
Bright notes
in white-out storms.

## LAST DAYS

*In memory of Bebe*

I could only think to give her bread.
What else to offer a woman

who has everything she needs
tucked into a valise of valor.

By her side, a good man who loves her
and two devoted dogs.

A hearth fire to settle by on chilly
autumn nights.

A bowl of heirloom tomatoes
fresh from the garden.

And those hens, *the girls*, that aerate
and operate the egg factory.

Once again to feel snowflakes
on her lashes at the cabin in Montana,

the warmth of morning coffee and a walk
in sunshine as bright as her smile.

So I bring her something simple
from my hands to hers:

cardamom bread braided
with my esteem

and hot cross buns
just in time for Easter;

each bun risen and marked
with the sign of peace.

## COFFEE BREAK

It was Christmastime,
the balloons needed blowing,
and so in the evening
we sat together to blow
balloons and tell jokes,
and the cool air off the hills
made me think of coffee,
so I said, "Coffee would be nice,"
and he said, "Yes, coffee
would be nice," and smiled
as his thin fingers pulled
the balloons from the plastic bags;
so I went for coffee,
and it takes a few minutes
to make the coffee
and I did not know
if he wanted cow's milk
or condensed milk,
and when I came out
to ask him, he was gone,
just like that, in the time
it took me to think,
cow's milk or condensed;
the balloons sat lightly
on his still lap.

# LATE FOR THEIR OWN FUNERALS
*for Leigh*

"Late for their own funerals,"
she'd joke, if she could see us,
her long-time friends, rushing across
the parking lot to hers. The smell of coffee
nearly does us in. We waver in the vestry,
absorb its welcome, its darker confirmation.

She's not among the women bustling below,
slicing squares onto sturdy platters, buttering
loaves of bread. There'll be a big crowd.
We lean toward their murmurs: "Sad.
Her family still so young."

Six months ago she'd been the busiest
butterer of all, loudest whisperer, first to hug.
Now she's the one being eulogized, lain
beneath a giant hand-hewn cross, likened to
St. Barnabas, encourager of all.

She's the one who should have been built
of thirty-foot beams, towering over mourners
who survive by luck, not good works. She must
be watching from her new elevation, silenced
for once, as we snuffle our way downstairs,
as we sip the coffee we so wanted her to share.

# SMALL TOWN COFFEE HOUSE

We don't know what to do.
We look at each other through a scrim of silence,
finger the thin hem of our understanding,
feel the frayed edge of heartbreak.

After the fog turned hard, after the shriek of steel,
the glitter of glass shards on the rain-slick road,
the hush of it everywhere.

How are we left with nothing but silence?
She didn't know when she left for work
that morning she would not arrive;
the young barista who always smiled
as she steamed our espressos
and the thing is
I didn't know her name.

Robin Amelia Morris

## HOLY PATENT HOLDER

It took four and a half million patents
before this disk emerged
to contain my coffee and keep it warm.

All those busy Americans
figuring out ways to improve on nature
and make a buck

off the billions who hold no shiny patent
(no, you can't see the reflection of panties
in this kind).

Someone holds a patent on the tool
which stamps the patent number
on the plastic lid of this coffee cup.

Oh Great Patent-Holder above,
who has provided each being
with an indescribable sense

of its own uniqueness
and centrality to the scheme,
if we should happen to discover

that birthmark back there is really a number,
let this knowledge sink
back into our cloudy dreams

and let our first slow sips of coffee
ferry us to some other sleep.

## ARTICULATED TRAM

By basement filigrees, the intricate particulars of passageways.
By looklongs in bank lobbies that lead to suspicions unresolved.
By alleys, lumbered with their Chinese restaurants, hung ducks,
    trouble-me packets—instant noodles.
By the dressmaker who sells stolen watches from her balcony
    because.
By the gypsy family who work the sidewalk where scents last,
    linger—ginger, Turkish coffee—just past opera crowds.
By a roman face surprised in the wall of a house. The butcher
    used the stall downstairs until police last summer
    roughed him up. His hands knew. His hands revealed
    sinews sublime with design.
By cocktail seminars—down-shops, really—where argument
    keeps seeping along the hallway.
By apartment blocs, whose weariness charms—think of such
    intrigues of the window-frame as it crumbles, its little
    cracks the cracks tracing through an old woman's
    memory.
By accidents, held to one's self, the suggestions.
By the equestrian statue luring, revolutions that finally won't
    matter.
By bookstores whose shelves display confused appliances.
    Toasters from Singapore. One curling iron. Leon Uris'
    monolithic *Trinity*.
By yellowgreen or purple houses—the elaborate wooden gates—
    still sobering under the sun.
By a briefcase and Italian suit.
By the ruins, remade. That stone, is it a widow's shawl? Her
    shadow looms still like the breath of a gesture.

With your permission, I will rise and note her going.

## MIRAGE

In the subway tunnel I see you—must be—
face the same size yours would be

at the same height. Hair as light.
But the mother holding your hand

is not right. A stain like spilled coffee crosses her face.
She stares straight back, making me sorry.

She thinks I am staring
at that.

# POEM FOR PAUL

Lately, crows have been invading poems,
those *hoi polloi* birds, irascible
and unashamed. An eye for the mystic
ordinary, Paul knew the difference
between crow and raven—*Most poem crows
are ravens*, he might say, pointing
out their size, their heavy bill,
their solitary strut.

While others scanned for kestrel
or for heron, Paul wondered about gulls,
their range and variations, their easiness
with all things human and the limitless,
inhuman sea. *An underrated bird*,
he might say.

For years in one small bedroom where
the sea could just be heard,
Paul held ongoing court for grownup
children, his beery Buddha's smile
traveling with them,
Moscow, Moose Jaw, Lhasa,
back with an unusual rock
or plastic wind-up toy for Paul
to slowly take in hand, consider,
comment on. His comment
the reward for the journey.

He wrote his poems on scraps
dropped in a coffee can
or sent on cards to friends,
no copy kept, or lost

in drifts around his bed.
One of the rare ones
who knew that the writing
is everything.
What happens after
doesn't matter.

Tom Hansen

## MOONSET

Standing in ankle-deep snow,
a mug of coffee cupped in gloved hands,
its dusky scent rising up,

I watch the moon tumble to earth
and disappear into its faraway grave
this last hour before daylight.

*The moon is dead, long live the moon,*
I hear myself silently sigh,
raising a cup, bitter and cold,

to praise and to mourn the great fallen moon,
whose dark downward journey
lights us our way.

# V.

# The Coffee Between Us

*He was my cream, and I was his coffee—*
*And when you poured us together, it was something.*

—Josephine Baker

## ITALIAN COFFEE

I stood up close under the eaves, impatient for Buddy to lift his leg on the first bush that smelled right. The rain felt familiar, felt like an English rain, intermittent yet insistent, faintly drumming the windows all afternoon. Two gray jays zipping from tree to tree remind me of the day I first met Rosie, freshly arrived in London from Florence to sharpen her English, and the flighty, fluttery motion of her hands: she speaks a cobbled mix of English and Italian—the Italian when English falls short of her feeling—waving a cigarette or shaking her finger to make a point. We stand in her kitchen. She grinds the coffee beans. I duck my head to pass under the bare light bulb. Now she brews espresso over the gas flame. "Italian coffee," she says, "you like some?" Sometimes in London, when the rain has let up, the wind blows fat drops out of the trees and it's almost raining again. Rosie's grin is big and toothy, frequent, a touch lewd. She has just asked, "What is a wanker?" and I answer with a flick of the wrist. Her laugh makes the silver hoops in her ears jiggle. She asks how to conjugate verbs like *fly* and *fuck*. She loves the word *percolate*. Tonight the deck reflects the yellow porch light in puddled water, the yard and what lies beyond quiet as I am, lost in this imagining—the patter of rain on a kitchen window, smell of coffee, steamed milk— quiet as Rosie in the long pause between opening her mouth and saying something—*anything*—in English. One afternoon, when the rain had stopped, she unlatched the window and told me all the ways an Italian could say my word *love*. The hush that followed fell like sunlight shafting past the open pane, the unsayable shining there between us.

# ANOMIA

Today I lost the name of a friend.
I looked in all the obvious places—under
the bed, behind the bookcase, in the junk drawer,
a potpourri of screws, batteries, and spare
birthday candles—*nada* . Looking at my
wachamacallit—the gizmo you tell time with—
I realized I had wasted half an hour looking
for the thing. Ridiculous! Call her Jane
and be done with it. I'll probably find it later
when I've forgotten about it.

My freckled hands reach for my old mug,
the one I bought somewhere or other (it was winter,
I think, snow on the ground…), the one where golden eagles
wing around the rim, the one I always drink
my coffee from since I don't know when. I see
Jane's forty-year-old face—right now—and smile,
listening to the way we talked and talked here
at the kitchen table, we told the kids we too
were playing, mommy games, they paused a moment, puzzled
over that, but quickly turned again to zooming
their hotwheels cars under and around our feet,
their *rmmm rmmming* threading through our conversation.
What did we talk about? No clue. But it was lovely.
Gossip, probably, and recipes, and tips
of the trade for getting over-tired toddlers to go
to sleep, and school systems, and a book she/I
had read, and a movie we might see if
we could get a babysitter. What books?
what movies? The details have escaped, down
the Dispose-All of the decades, as the children lifted
off with their still-smooth skin and brown hair
into their grown-up lives. But those afternoons

with Jane—Janet? Jenny? find their way into
the handle of my coffee cup, gone now,
but still warm. Still warm.

# MORNING

The hesitant gait, slow
focus, the T-shirt I wore
as pajamas, the hair dried
in sleep now a derangement
of curls and horns

drifting down the hall
to the breakfast room,
with decaf, humdrum,
or bold, instant
oatmeal, pastries, patties
or links

and eggs little beds lined up
or scrambled
like a traveler's brain

the TV a whirl of rising
waters, spreading flames,
volcanic instability,
impropriety, the fear
of private public lands

ratings and the latest
in black-cherry
fingernail design.

I miss my little grandson
already, his life bright
with giggles and tears,
not yet walking, pure reaction
to hunger and explosive glee.

It's time for me now, the sun
upbeat, the shadows bold,
to check out with a map
and coffee, then contemplate
the best way home.

I couldn't find the mushrooms under the begonias in the garden, then I remembered I had seen them growing there in a dream. The flowering thistle, dewdrops clinging to the spider's web—it wasn't all a dream. That's coffee I smell, not wood smoke; and here's the glass vial where my wife has saved all our children's teeth.

# WAKING ELSEWHERE

I woke up dreaming my mother's garden—
fields in autumn, green turning gold,
grasses scythed down in the late, dark sun;
and here will be corn, she was saying, tomatoes,
flowers I never knew she loved.

I woke to a child climbing into my bed
—four-year-old girl of my sister's son—
hair like silk and the color of wheat
falling into her eyes, begging me to get up.

And in my mother's kitchen the strong light smelled of coffee
and autumn, in fact. In fact, my mother,
who hasn't gardened in twenty years, was taking a bath.
I heard her splashing through the walls. It was October;
the child came forward, one fresh egg cupped in her palm.

I woke up dreaming the harrowed fields,
sharp with stubble, my mother's lands.
She was already preparing for spring; she was already
stepping naked from the bath, away from grief—

a widow with work to do, weeds in the yard,
and the child calling softly to me, *come on, come on, come on.*

# FLIGHT

My mother's dreams were dreams of her children being carried away by a storm. Six of us—where was the seventh? —tied by our waists with a rope to her waist; a daisy-chain of bodies too light to land, we unfurled in the wind. She said it was always spaghetti that kept her awake. She said Italian food spelled nightmares and my father used to work those tepid hours until dawn. How was I blessed to never know my mother was so afraid?

Until one morning I crept out and saw them sitting on the front steps of the house, the light still gray above their heads. My mother in her flowered summer duster and my father in his uniform, dark blue. She must have called him home from work; he must have come—leaving the noise of the runway, the silver monsters we all loved, the DC9's, the cargo planes, the tools so certain in his hands—just to hold her while she cried. To whisper here like this: *Shhh, the kids are all in bed. They'll be all right.*

All but one, who was standing there watching through the screen door, terrified, loved. Knowing that anything could happen, suddenly; knowing the clock on the stove was turned to a time I couldn't tell. Dream time. Their coffee cups. And the way she fit like a blossom into the blossom of his arms. And how I felt the nightmare wind already coming up and couldn't warn them, and how weightless I've become.

Sharry Phelan Wright

# NORTH CASCADES' MORNING

The trick, my father said, is eggshells,
crushed and tossed into the pot
to settle out the grounds.
He called it cowboy coffee—
mild, lucent and slightly gritty.
We singed our tongues, watched
mist like downy feathers lift
off the surface of the alpine lake
that cold and copper morning.

Both quiet people, easy in a place
where quiet was a rite, we left babble
to the white-barked pines, the hush of wind,
the fee-bee, fee-bee call of chickadees.
Resting in that nest of wood and water,
light and stone, we sat on logs,
navigated scrambled eggs from dented metal plates,
the tip-tap scratch of spoons a form of blessing
in a newly coded language,
that last summer before my leaving home.

Down at the water's edge, I washed my face
in the frigid lake, my image fraying out
in scattered ribbons, the clouds inside me sinking
to the bottom with the smooth, round stones
shaped over time by glaciers. After, we broke camp
and walked back down the mountain,
leaving, along with a bit of buried tissue,
scattered crumbs and a small mound of eggshells
mixed in with cowboy coffee grounds.

D. R. James

## REASSURANCE TO MY FUTURE SPOUSE

You may not know me yet,
but I'm learning just who you must be,

trusting you're getting ready
for the rest of our lives.

Perhaps you're already emptying
several mental drawers, clearing psychic

spaces for another razor, another coffee cup,
disrobing the slender shoulders

of a dozen wooden hangers
in the scented closet of your subtle heart.

Don't worry, I'm not voyeuristic—
not strictly speaking anyway—

though I have been watching your
comings and goings—goings, mostly—

in the sector labeled *maybe* in my mind.
And you've surely bided your sweet time,

perhaps sometimes willingly, or unwillingly
as I, waiting for the grip on our two fates—

on our two lines of blind perspective—
to converge at that distant but critical point

where we collide, then teeter, then tip
over an imagined ledge, falling, finally,

hopelessly into love. Meanwhile,
I'm enjoying the way the wind

will want to splay stray strands of hair
across your face as you pose for a corny photo

by a springtime pond, and how the waves
of your dear body, the surf

of your complicated soul, will form
and conform to the shores of mine—

and how this will work just as perfectly
the other way around.

D. R. James

## LOVE BUZZ
*for Suzy*

The coffee's made for, what,
the thirty-five-hundredth time?
Give or take. For a decade,
in four months. *Love Buzz!*
We joke, but that nails it,
and not just the coffee. Lord,
the buzz she brews in me.
Nights, too much streamed TV,
then the old novel I'm reading
dips for the fifth time. We say
"Click" when we spoon, the
ten-year ritual still a perfect fit.

## AFTER YOU

Before bed you grind the beans near fine,
and set the timer for our daily regime
of drip, sip and go.
The maker is up before we are,
is up with the towhees, the brown birds
*peeping* their way through the yard
as liquid gurgles and flows.
Another alarm.
It works out to be about a pound each week.
Whole beans bought in 12oz bags
at the local third-wave café.
Unless we order from the desert roaster
in bulk, five pounds at a time.
Each morning, an intoxicating scent
fills the kitchen, fills the carafe,
the next thing reached for, after you.

# DAWN STIRRING

Your amethyst voice cloaks the morning mint and cream
as you gift me a cup of coffee,
fresh pressed for my sleepy hands
naked on the pillow.

I nose the rim
sip my daily dose
let the steam tickle my eyelids
heavy with breaking sunshine.

You prop on the door jam,
white ceramic idle at the end of one arm,
your eyes lit blue with all their fire like witch twilight.

I reach for your everyday fingers,
your skin on mine a sharper stimulant
than anything you brew.

## SATURDAY MORNING

I often wish I were an artist
on Saturday mornings,
coffee in the pot
discreetly steaming,
a bookmark in the volume
you've been reading,
the *Times* scattered
about the living room floor,
and all crises of the week
solved or averted.

I'd set up my easel
quietly near a window
and spread colors
on my palette, lots of blue
and lighthearted pastels,
a pale yellow for the sun
emerging in the east.

I'd skim the canvas lightly
with the tip of the brush,
sweep in the curves
and with careful strokes
strive for the perfect depiction
of that moment of magic.

Though it would take a Renoir,
perhaps a Monet or Vermeer,
to capture the focus
and pure Saturday morning
serenity of you...

sitting barefoot
and deep in thought
in a lotus position

in your overstuffed chair,
sipping hot black coffee
from your favorite mug,

penciling numbers onto a page
of Sudoku squares,
occasionally pausing,
eyebrows bunched,
to scrub your eraser
till a hole tears into the paper.

## MOCHA LATTE

I know by the rugged tone of your voice
how you feel
                    at this particular moment
when red streaks fill the evening sky—
a sign for tomorrow's sunshine.

Your voice travels across peaks and lows,
pausing for quick articulation, searching for
that specific term
          that defines your ever-changing philosophy.

Not that I mind, not at all. I love to listen
to your chatter. Your pitch goes
up and down
                    to the sides
                              all over
          while background noises fade away.

I remember times of silence. Darkness.
Insecurity. Resentment.
But these have passed like a tropical storm.
You calmed down, matured, seasoned.

Your face shines when we meet.
We embrace losses.

At times, you laugh, sipping Mocha latte
(your favorite),
as we practice people watching.

Anne Graue

## DRINKING COFFEE IN
## OCCUPIED CYPRUS

It won't happen in your lifetime;
I won't sip from the muddy demitasse
the bitter dregs left for your mother to read
my fortune revealed in the legs
and patterns of powder still in the cup—
I can't go that far.

I hear the water in Famagusta is so blue
it is painful to look at for too long.

We took pictures of the guard tower in '87
on the green line in Nicosia—
resolution for replacing Greek families
with Turkish ones.

You explained that the coffee was Turkish,
a relic from the Ottomans,
a reminder that the Island of Aphrodite
had occupiers before, has changed

hands so many times it barely knows
itself. You were a hero to me, enduring
solitary during your military service
for thanking your commanding officer
for noticing you lacked the military mentality.

We turned the car around at the green line
after a night with friends from Queens,
our 8-month-old daughter asleep—
my eyes wide; my lips and arms taut
at the sight of guns; UN peacekeepers
did not seem so peaceful.

188

But what did I know?

After 25 years, you still ask if I want
Greek coffee—knowing I'll refuse
the bitter sweetness, the thickened
dust that sinks to the bottom
of every cup standing next to a *tavli*
board in Kyrenia or Limassol,
where the coffee is Turkish
and has been for so long.

# iCONTACT
*(Another love poem for my husband)*

Your cowlick, once dark and rich like java
shimmers like snow on a mountain-top,
highlights gleaming in morning sun
slanting in through the breakfast-room window
where you sit in your flowered chair,
head bowed over the news.

It reminds me of the time we climbed
Mt. Washington, in October of '84,
when a winter storm dumped half a foot
and we woke in our camp on the mountainside
to a broken MSR stove, not enough warm clothes,
worst of all, no coffee.

I followed you to the summit that day,
even though you left me in the boulder fall
when we lost the trail, because
who couldn't love
your insouciance—your over-the-shoulder
"See you at the top"—or sex in a frigid tent,
or the way your hazel eyes
keep changing color
like autumn leaves?

Sipping my coffee, I ask you to look
at the sun. I want to see
if your eyes have faded,
like the upholstery
on your favorite chair,
but you don't respond.

I make a face across the rim of my kitty-cat mug
and silently curse the top of your head

along with all things Apple, but
you swipe your screen and ignore
my glare
and my voice streaming past your ear.

My favorite part of the morning comes
with the ding of a message received:

If your iPhone had a vagina,
we'd be divorced.

## RAZONES PARA COMPRAR
## CAFÉ ON LINE

Y no te olvides de comprar café,
Me dices
en un whatsapp
a las siete y diez de la mañana.
Yo estoy -como siempre- de viaje
y tú atiendes la casa
y a los niños
y me digo: Qué dicha
de esta normalidad.
Falta café en un sitio
a dos mil cuatrocientas
millas de distancia
y corro a abrir la página del súper
y a ponerle remedio
encargando el café que más nos gusta:
natural, nunca en grano,
paquete grande como nuestra suerte,
tamaño ahorro, lo que significa
que el segundo paquete cuesta menos.
Una vez el café ya está en camino
ambos sabemos
lo que eso significa:
Habrá más sobremesas de domingo
frente a tazas que humean,
pequeños sorbos de palabras,
nuestras conversaciones sin destino ni objeto,
Inútiles
como el deseo que pervive
como el ansia de estar aquí, charlando,
un domingo tras otro.

Care Santos
Lawrence Schimel (translator)

## REASONS TO BUY
## COFFEE ONLINE

And don't forget to buy coffee,
you tell me
in an SMS
at seven ten a.m.
I am (like always) on a trip
and you're taking care of the house
and the kids
and I tell myself: This normality
is wonderful.
Coffee is lacking somewhere
two thousand four hundred
miles away,
and I rush to open the supermarket's website
and remedy the situation,
ordering the coffee we like best:
natural, already-ground,
the large
super-saver size, which means
that the second package costs less.
Once the coffee is now on its way
we both know
what that means:
There will be more lazy Sunday post-meal chats
over steaming mugs,
small sips of words,
our conversations without any goal or aim,
useless,
like the desire that endures,
like the yearning to be here, talking,
Sunday after Sunday.

Con mucho que decir
a pesar de que lo hemos dicho todo.
El café nos promete un sorbo más
de vida cotidiana,
en que tú y yo seremos tú y yo
sin ruido ni golpes.
La vida pasará sobre el café
igual que pasa el tiempo,
a toda prisa.
Y si amarguea mucho
tú añadirás azúcar a mi taza
y yo a la tuya
como siempre solemos,
con la cursilería que acompaña al amor
y que ve todo el mundo
menos el par de ciegos que la sufren.
Antes de cerrar la web del súper
me digo que aquí,
a dos mil cuatrocientas millas de distancia,
el café es un amarre
a la vida que quise.
Un espejismo que me dice:
Aunque acabe mañana
tu suerte ya es eterna.

With lots to say
despite our having already said everything.
The coffee promises us another sip
of everyday life,
in which you and I will be you and I
without noise or blows.
Life will pass over the coffee
just as time passes,
in a rush.
And if it gets too bitter
you'll add sugar to my mug
and I to yours
like we usually do,
with the cloying cuteness that accompanies love,
visible to everyone
but that blinded couple who suffer from it.
Before closing the supermarket's webpage
I tell myself that here,
two thousand four hundred miles away,
the coffee is an anchor
to the life I wanted.
A mirage that tells me:
Even should it end tomorrow
your luck is already eternal.

You are all caramel bones
liquor on your breath,
strong-brew coffee
in the morning,
glitter-eyes on sleepless nights and
alcohol-induced mistakes
under cloudy Dublin nights;
don't mind
bitter aftertastes
drown it down
more coffee, more you.

Love love love is all we need,
Darling, don't mind my tears
in the night; the bloodshot eyes
"without you, I am empty" I said,
whispered into a silent night.
I hit the ground running, flying.
We are like night and day and
love always ends in tragedies.

Diane Stone

# HOW TO FELL AN ALDER

First you need a spouse
to tell you not to do it.
But of course you must do it.
That old tree drops dead wood
on the main path to the barn—
sways above the wood shed,
reminds you of tasks
you didn't finish or even start.

You make a pot of coffee
and review the whole plan:
Extension ladder, pruning saw,
steel cable, old Sears chainsaw
to oil, coddle, crank.

The tree stands tall, green
and leafy, an honest soldier.
In that moment between felling
and not felling, resolve shifts
as if your own deep roots
have lost their grip. You feel
too much a part of these woods
to add one more slash
of destruction.
Take a deep breath.

When the tree crashes down
just where you planned it,
triumph isn't what you feel;
regret maybe, even remorse.

## OUR HOUSE

*"I thought about you and about the emptiness*
*that can promise one thing only: plenitude"*
—Adam Zagajewski, "Balance"

I walked through the gutted interior
and thought of scaffolding: truthful scaffolding.
I observed wooden beams and tufts of pink
fiberglass that surrounded us as we slept.

I thought about you and about solidity
which offers one thing only—dissolution—
and saw how ruined castles
sprang from our famous secrets.

Stones and plaster were smoothed
over eruptions and mundane routine
began again: the perk of coffee,
the clink of wineglasses.

Secrets crept back into mouse holes
undetected by vigilant cats.

Joel Brouwer

## COFFEE AND ORANGES

The music on TV turned gloomy. Sharks,
she said, and sure enough. A blunt snout,
jumbled cemetery of teeth, and quick black
depthless eye thrashed the screen. Coffee
and oranges made the morning acidic.
She said, the cello is the instrument
of the inevitable. White clouds
of jasmine devoured a trellis. He said,
no, the cello is an instrument of caution.
And with that they splashed overboard into
the swells and chop and chum and his lust
for control took dominion everywhere,
like a shark, like he fucked, always either
much too much or nothing at all. He said
he'd make her a deal. If she could face
the mirror a hundred mornings straight and
say out loud she wanted one and mean it
she could have a child. That wasn't bad
enough. Six days later he came off in her
without a condom. And wanted to hug
and cry about it. Brought a warm washcloth.
Said she'd misunderstood. Was this
fate or warning? Punishment or praise?
She didn't even ask; she understood
he didn't understand the difference.
She idled in the Rite Aid parking lot,
adding the omen of the stiff kitten
near the dumpster to the omen of the goth girl
flashing past on her skateboard with a bright
pink bubble perched in her mouth. Called it
a draw. Tore up the prescription and drove
home to coffee, oranges, the inevitable
cello. A hundred mornings and no telling
on which the shark will or won't rip

her open, turn the bitter pith and grounds
of her insides out. The music might warn her
but the shark never will. She's gone. She's here.

# INSTANT WAS ALL WE HAD

We wake in the shadows like morning clouds
Quickened by the blanching of our gunpowder joe,
The bitterness in its groundless bite somewhat leavened
By the creamless milk or milkless creams or whatever synthetic
Fancy might otherwise grace our graceless hands, listening,
Perhaps, for birdcalls or countbells or the silent drams
Held within our partner's unknowing snore, the one we'd prefer,
At least until we've had our way with the morning news

And secured the last and secret nibbles of the secret
Pastries we've had to reconcile with the mirror we pretend
No one else must ever know, like when we feel we must
So carefully fold the unseen wrappers and hide them
Beneath the unsearched and unrecyclable bits like the last
Origamic question we'd rather not give than know.

Uma Venkatraman

## STORM IN A COFFEE CUP

Morning breaks
into my coffee cup
brew made bitter
by the sludge of
last night's fight
Heat of your words
still lingers in each sip
I should have picked tea
and read the leaves
to reveal tomorrow

Joy Valerius

## COFFEE AFICIONADO
*for Elizabeth Brunt*

You chomp down
on coffee beans

as if they were
candy.

They create a
thunder in you,

and send lightning
all around you.

You start over
the next morning

like Rover playing
ball,

unable to stop.

Your dance with coffee
continues

long into the evening.

## MORNING COFFEE

At the bar she asked the tender:
"Is this a good night
to meet someone?"
"No," he said, "things pick up
later in the week."

So she went home again with Lucky.

It was not the sex that made her queasy
        (she was a good athlete and never lost composure)
but morning coffee, the intimate hour,
looking at his lime-green shirt,
        his oily hair,
looking at her watch, again.

## BED SONG

Like smooth, creamy coffee on a slow Sunday morning
oh Lord fuck me again.

The caramel ribbons of your voice,
make of them a sling for all that ails me.

The bone-rocking dark-breaking staggering
abundance behind my eyelids
fragments into a million shards of sound.

I slink into this light of stars I've loved too much to fear;
the darkness like a tiger in jungled dappling,
like the grace of a caged bird

set suddenly free. You stain your fingers
on my pomegranate seeds, you pluck the chords of
my mandolin like a boy plucks a nickel from a creek;

spit-shine and polish my cadmium. I the fever
and you the alkali—remedy, cure and antidote
to the self-same venom injected in my blood fruit.

Every time you go to the *kavárna*, I ask for decaf
but you bring me leaded *káva*.

All the buzz inherent in a beehive.
When I leave, I take your honey just the same.

## MEASURING WATER BY SOUND

I want to know the color of your eyes, not just the browns
and greens of them, but by the specific Pantone colors of
their constellations.

I want to know by rote how your tongue forms the syllables
of my name, the way your lips make words in the dark.

I want to know your skin like I know my favorite sweater,
how it caresses my shoulders, hugs my hips…where it rests
against my belly.

I want to know you by sound, the way I know I've poured
enough water in the pot for coffee we'll drink by moonlight
at 3.

# BESO DEL DIABLO

It was just chocolate cake, special
only by virtue of the spice
it was laced with, the *certain effect*
the waiter only hinted at, with a broad grin
and a coy cautionary gesture. We heard him out
on other choices, but our course had been set—
one slice, two forks, and a strong Spanish
coffee for you. The conspiratorial look
men exchange on such occasions
passed from him to you to him with that dark
sustenance, its effect on me
uncertain. Over the last bite
of our oversexed dessert, you regaled
our friends with the tale of our cross-
country move—the truck, the diesel
fuel, your *butch points*. After the last kiss
of our private dessert, we whisper, wonder how
such passion could ignite *sans* the flame
of two hearts, four breasts, that certain
curve of hip no man could claim.
Where are those butch points now?
Perhaps they pepper the dessert plate,
placid among the spiced chocolate crumbs
and two forks smeared by the kiss
of the Devil.

## COFFEE STAIN

you told me
my coffee colored eyes
were anything but
boring,
and yet you are there and i am here
so much distance spread against
the tapestry of us that the
stars can barely align in those positions
for wincing;
yet i remember everything
clear as day
as if it were yesterday—
first, it was pleasurable,
we burned like the leaves of autumn
full of passion and grace
then suddenly you were the hot of coffee thrown
upon my lap searing as the sharp edge
of the fangs of wolves;
you were snarling and swiping at me
nothing i could say would sway you because you
had already decided i was too intense and too strong—
a weak man could not carry the weight of me
so it was probably good for you to get
out while you could,
but you did it in the worst possible way
so i pray every sunset of my eyes still burns you
until eternity delivers you to void.

## MILKY COFFEE

Usually I don't want sugar in my coffee
but today I pour in a spoonful
and there it is, memory in sweet coffee.
I am fifteen, riding in the back seat
of an old Plymouth driven by Art,
my friend Bonnie's father,
because it's late at night and she is too tired
to drive back from Portland to Coos Bay,
and I am too young to drive at all.
The night before, Art, a kind but broken man,
pulled himself together after we found him
at his favorite tavern in Portland.
I waited on the sidewalk
under a streetlight with moths circling
and Bonnie, twenty-one, went in to get him.
Now, shaky but clean, Art sits at the wheel.

Bonnie wants to start her own business
raising night crawlers in a dirt box
back of the auto court, down
by the slough where we both live.
She says we will sell them to fishermen
and make easy money.
Yesterday we counted out
ten thousand night crawlers on a farm
up on Prune Hill, outside Camas.
Now, with a trailer on the back of the Plymouth
we're taking them home.
There's dense fog from Otis Junction south,
not just fog but midnight fog
where you can't see the curve of the road
until you're in it. On our left I glimpse
leaning from the rocky bank
salal, monkey flowers, stunted coastal pines,

but in this fog I can't see the ocean
far below on the right.
Now as we drive south I fall asleep.
That's what fifteen-year-olds do.
And we go through dark and fog until
we stop somewhere, maybe Depoe Bay,
at an all-night café
on the east side of the highway.
I don't drink coffee yet but tonight
I order a cup as Bonnie and Art do.
I fill my bitter cup with cream and sugar.
a lot of it, so it's sweet and milky, then sip.
I'd never known coffee was this good.

I hold it, hot, with both hands, and as I drink,
something is etched on my mind,
something sweet and milky, something
along with the feeling of being lost
in the fog of life, but exciting too.
Taste of milky coffee and the thought
*someday I will be someone*
come all at once. Later the fog clears.
Deep as the ocean that wafts and purls offshore
as we drive south, expectation, sweet coffee,
sweet milky memory, like all the rest,
settles down in me.

Edwina Trentham

# MORNINGS WHEN MY SISTER
# USED TO FLY

She would haul me, dull-eyed
with sleep, from my rumpled
sheets, fold my fingers
around a crumpled shirt, point
me into darkness, long before sunrise
whispered pink at the black horizon.

Creeping down stone steps, I'd yank
the length of knotted string, set
the bare bulb to sweeping shaky
pinwheels of light through cobwebs,
as I leaned to plug the cord,
counting to twenty, tapping the tip

of my finger on metal,
before slamming steam
into collars and armpits,
nosing heat around
buttonholes, across cuffs, up
and down wrinkled sleeves.

Yawning, jaw cracking,
I'd moan for my cooling sheets
as my sister hissed *hurry*, scampered
down to snatch her shirt. Later,
slumped in school, I would imagine
her stalking narrow rows of seats,

narrow rows of blank faces,
reaching for dirty glasses,
wine, coffee staining the shirt
she would wash late that night,
knowing I'd still be a fool
for love next morning.

## COFFEE

I loved it immediately like cigarettes or scotch.
I was 14 in a diner with a boy.
It came black and steaming in a thick china mug.
He asked if I wanted cream or sugar.
I sipped it straight, it was exactly what I wanted.
My mother percolated Maxwell House in a cheap
Metal pot. She never offered it to me until I asked.
Like when I told her I smoked; then she
Opened her pack of Camels. I said I preferred
Chesterfields.

So coffee and cigarettes.
The acrid odor of a Zippo lighter. The small sharp wheel
I thumbed. Or the carbon strike of a match on a black strip
Of stiffened paper.
That was grown-up.
Like the roadhouse outside Roundup
Where a hand was purple-stamped and pints of cheap
Whiskey poured into flasks. Then we danced
To the cowboy band.

So coffee. That's where it started.
A thick black brew.
In time, I learned to grind
Arabic beans. Invested in an expensive machine
With complex settings. That's how you start a day.
Coffee.

Still, nothing beats the taste of that first cup
With its gritty residue
And a boy watching me intently,
Seeing how I liked it.

Deborah Meltvedt

## COFFEE EVOLUTION

You start with mom
7th grade
morning paper and just a little
bit of Sweet N Low
You won't know it yet
but you are trying to lose
weight before you knew
what pounds meant
before anyone would ever
call you fat.

In high school you live
on halves of cheeseburgers
and gulps of Folgers in
white styrofoam cups.
You won't know it yet
but you are disappearing
before anyone knew to ask
how you liked your coffee
or how you liked
anything at all.

The summer you turn 18 you
are hooked on Denny's booths
and Salem Lights, staring out on
Blackstone avenue, at tanned
boys in fast cars.
We don't know it yet but
the boys are not for us and
when you come home with
a burn in your skirt, your
mother says *don't judge her*
but pours you one more cup,
only not once, not once
do you light each other's light.

213

In college you work as a barista
before you knew that baristas were a job.
You make good foam and yell
*Rick double Latte!* before you
know you will kiss him in a
storm where you feel as visible
as lightning and hotter than any
shot you've ever made.

You make good foam before
you know you will marry
*Rick double Latte!* and your
mother will dance at your
wedding and drink champagne,
not coffee. You have no idea
that one year later your mother
will ask for just one sip
*one sip!*
of lukewarm St. Agnes coffee
you cannot give her
as her lips sucks ice and her
lungs forget to breathe.
And this is when you never
Realized—
you could do without.
So the two of you just sit,
without a light or a cup

Just sit.

Until she disappears and
*Rick double Latte!* brings you
something warm and black
to help you forget what
you knew was coming all
along, and to remember
what came before.

## TOSSING COFFEE

When peering across the seminar table
at the young man with a silver moon ring
and model's jawline, you never imagine
he's capable of reducing you to a simpering teen
or raising you up at his whim. You come to crave
his stoic observations, how he namedrops
Heidegger and Nietzsche, come to love
his rare compliments about you. You accept
his French-pressed coffee, wrap your hands
around the Denby mug crafted in England,
one of a set of mismatched elegance, smell
the earthy chocolate of Sumatra beans roasted
for a charming local shop downtown
that you visit weekly after driving
thirty minutes from country to city in his silver car
that always has the windows down, even
in winter, chilling your knuckles and nose
on the Skyway, music too loud for talk,
which is fine because driving always puts him
into one of his fierce moods and you may as well
be a bobblehead metronome on the dash
keeping his stormy company until you arrive
at the trendy restaurant with aloof employees
and you eat the omelet with crisp bacon and oozing cheese
he will later blame for your pudginess, and instead
of upending that grass green and mud brown mug
onto his otherwise cheap coffee table,
you think of the last time on the highway
when he cut off a pickup truck and it soared
down the on-ramp beside you to toss
a full, steaming cup of coffee onto the hood
of his car and the fury pulsing in his neck
when he swore in disbelief at the rain of drops.
Still brings a smile to your lips.

# FRENCH COFFEE

he brewed it thick and dark
my lover
in that two-chair rented kitchen
where a single rose
in a cracked clay pot
bloomed pink
outside the twice-locked door

January in
Marseilles
keeps blue shutters firmly closed
and steady stench
of bitter cigarettes
can find
nowhere to escape

I thought I would be safe
with him
I thought he'd be the same sane man
I'd met and kissed
as soft August sun
ripened slow
hard red blackberries

beer and beer and beer
through midnight
rage and hate and grief since childhood
tightening
his trembling hands
stained brown
with years of nicotine

he tore to shreds the poems
I wrote
he slapped me hard to make me cry
at being nothing
but a weak woman
worthless
in his anguished eyes

I pretended I
agreed
I kept my passport safely hid
and when he went
to buy more smokes
I pushed
the window free and fled

## OFFERING A CUP

I can't figure out why the coffee turns bitter.
The coffee pots have varied from glass
to aluminum to coated copper and still
the taste is once removed from vicious.

I've sniffed the grounds, bought bags
of different brands, tried egg shells
and boiling on the stove in both stainless
and stain-spotted pots, but the coffee

makes me twinge and shudder and the dog's tail
of my tongue whimpers, tucks, and runs.
My water's not chemically laced
nor mineral rich—I've had the tap tested, twice,

but the coffee's my nemesis, adversary,
hostile, harsh, not the social warmth
a host extends to a neighbor, yet Gary is
looking at the dregs in the bottom of a cup

not flinching, not cringing, smacking his lips
not out of satisfaction but to relieve
the scream the taste buds started, and I,
eyes wandering, trying not to look.

Once, I took his cat to the vet to take
the little life that cancer had left.
We've cleared waterways together
in the dark deluges of winter

with flashlights strapped to our heads.
We've lopped pear trees, yanked
scotch broom, fixed an old lady's fence.
He'll ask for another cup, never wince.

## SLIP/CRACK

The space between the mattress
      and the box spring is where we keep
remembrances of hushed
sycophants
idle worshipers
those who were lost and
those who could not stay

Slip grapefruit juice onto the
      bedside table for when I wake, you
are tired of many things, the
percolating coffee machine is one of them
ineptitude another
your daily commute, and
waiting, waiting, waiting the last, you
are never there when I awake

## NO MATTER

Folded close,
as mysterious as a rose, as love's poem
set to open, the cosmos waits

to blaze again, to shape itself
inside my head an Everywhere, the never-
ending unbeginning Everything

we're mirrored in. Twinned
and neither here nor there, the two of us
can sing the one old song back new.

Over coffee in a coffee shop
you'd seemed to ask if I'd try it all again.
I tried to ask why not?

We are our worlds, existence
is our wording of the lonely world of love.
They say—or we say they say—

of heaven's every star-wreathed
sphere and disk, every spiral out and fire-
fall back to ice:

no matter. The folding up
of even time and space unfolds another
mystery, another rose.

## REUNION

Our coming together again,
years after coming of age,
takes place on my home ground.
Over a table, we square off,
warm our hands on steaming cups
of coffee. You say I look the same.
I look at you, your face a foreign country
on which I trace the inroads made
by age and circumstance
and don't know what to say.
I tell you I cheated a bit at the surgeon's:
no reason why a lady ought to spend
the last two decades of her life
with a strong personality
and a weak chin.

You are still a mystery.

You let me prattle on about the trivial.
I find out later, when you've gone,
that you were in a war,
while I was only in a revolution,
the sexual one.

I want to know where you live.
I need to see the furniture
you've fitted to your life, since,
as the poet said, all's changed, utterly.
And inasmuch as it's too late for remedies
at any rate, why can't you show me,
in the picture frames I think
must line your hall,

your children, children's children,
accoutrements that separate
your life from mine?

Between us, all this time.
And on your wall,
the years we could have had.

## SWEET TOOTH

I dreamt of decadent dark chocolate,
rich savor of seventy-two percent cacao.
But you were only spun sugar
twirled on my tongue,
or licked from sticky fingers,
melting in my mouth.
You were pieces of candy for the mind
with fantasy lives of their own
that preoccupied me
like my tongue probing a missing tooth.
Still, I hold a place for the occasional
fleeting rush of cotton candy memories
dissolving in nothingness on my mind's tongue.

You never satisfied like warm bread,
the staff of my life.
Your listening did not midwife
parts of me I hadn't known.
You did not sustain me,
or offer love enduring as a redwood,
*sequoia sempervirens*,
whose concentric rings hold forever
the record of a relationship, rich
with rocky years and smooth.

But now I realize you offer
deep French roast's
tantalizing aroma,
fulfilling promise of a pick-me-up.
Friendship fresh brewed
again and again over years
cup by heartwarming
sixteen-ounce cup.

George Perreault

## COFFEE WITH MARY KATE

My lover, years ago, said her friend,
on finding I never drink coffee, thought
she shouldn't trust a man who could start
a morning like that, and my lover found this
funny until finally I broke her heart.

She works these days at a liberal church
in a college town surrounded by a country
which has strip-mined our dreams,
lobotomized our schools, bloated the prisons
and abandoned our sick to the leeches.

I wish her well in her last days' ministry
to the hungry and the maimed, while at this
next border I'm just hoping the remnants
of my family can pass the screening for
our homeland's zika of the soul.

Small mercies, my lover might say, small
mercies are all that's left, this kind curate
handing over a cup of joe while the jackals
scour the wreckage hoping to keep any gold
they've pried from the teeth of the dead.

# THE INTERVIEW

Tell me about the time
before you knew it all,
when you were just starting out
buying the things you needed.

Peel away the layers
of what you want me to think
and just talk.
Talk about the shoes,

the light-colored sweater,
the roses, the small roses you
said spilled over the fence.
Tell me about the first kiss,

the way it felt.
You knew from then on
that kisses stopped things
like STOP signs, because if I remember, you said

that's when you knew that
life wasn't going to be a series of
forwards, instead more
backwards than forwards.

At the end of your life
if you're lucky you'll be
right where you started, in the beginning,
with the sun and water.

Tell me about the coffee
with your mother and father
before school and the square of sugar.
Speak slowly.

# RAIN

Summer nights after our shift
Marilyn, Theresa and I sit on
the bench outside the ER.

We sip cold coffee, smoke,
watch the big dipper
refuse to burn out.

Stubborn as Sam Morgan's
stiff lungs coughing years
of mill dust. They will not die,

but can not live. Can this
be the same sky that bowed
to Cleopatra? Tormented Van Gogh?

We are nurses, not Shaman,
we whisper what we know.
Our daughters swim faster

than this moon, our sons' faces
are passengers in train windows,
every half second, science invents

gizmos for us to memorize,
red alarms, green beeps, chants
to raise the dying. We are plain

gray doves that will fly
from this bench the way tide
leaves the shore. Others will come,

sponges to bathe the lonely,
webs to bandage the angry.
One day, we will leave

this world, overnight
we'll become the rain.

# CONTRIBUTOR BIOGRAPHIES

**Debra Andrea Ahrens** fell in love with words after seeing her poem published on the chalkboard of her first-grade classroom. She has devoted many years to teaching young children the joy of reading, especially those who had to work harder to be successful. She started her coffee habit by drinking the nasty, overboiled brew that is ubiquitous in teacher's workspaces across the country, but now prefers to grind her own beans.

**Cynthia Rausch Allar** received her MFA in Writing in 2004. The poems written at Spalding University would never have happened without the blessings of coffee, for both early morning wake-ups and late-night writing at a coffee bar. She has been published in anthologies such as *Myrrh, Mothwing, Smoke* from Tupelo Press and the Cancer Poetry Project, as well as journals *Evening Street Review, Off the Rocks, Bloom, New Millennium Writings*, and others.

"Beso del Diablo" was previously published in the Winter 2011 issue of *Naugatuck River Review.*

**Elizabeth (Betsy) Aoki** completed her MFA at the University of Washington. She has received grants and fellowships from the City of Seattle, Artist Trust Foundation, Jackstraw Writers Program, and residencies at Hedgebrook and Clarion West. Her publications include the chapbook *Every Vanish Leaves Its Trace* by Finishing Line Press, and the Asian American female poets anthology *Yellow as Turmeric, Fragrant as Cloves.*

**Lana Hechtman Ayers** resides in the Pacific Northwest which is famous for two of the things she adores most in this world—coffee and rain. She is the author of 9 poetry collections and a time travel novel.

"Stoop-Sitting with Daddy" appears in Lana's full-length collection *The Dead Boy* (2018).

**Roxanne Barbour** is a Burnaby (Canada) novel writer of science fiction, mystery, adventure, and romance (often in the same manuscript): *Revolutions* (Whiskey Creek Press, 2015), *Sacred Trust* (Whiskey Creek Press, 2015), *Kaiku* (self-published, 2017), *Alien Innkeeper* (The Wild Rose Press, 2017), *An Alien Perspective* (self-published, 2017), *An Alien Confluence* (self-published, 2019). Roxanne is also exploring speculative poetry, with poems appearing in *Scifaikuest*, *Star\*Line*, and *Three Line Poetry*, and was the Featured Poet in the February 2018 issue of *Scifaikuest*.

**Ellen Bass** is a Chancellor of the Academy of American Poets. Her most recent book is *Like a Beggar*. Her poetry frequently appears in *The New Yorker*, *The American Poetry Review*, and many other journals. She teaches in the MFA writing program at Pacific University. She began drinking coffee as a child—weak Maxwell House with milk—because her mother thought it was good to have a warm drink in the morning. www.ellenbass.com

"Poem Written in the Sixth Month of My Wife's Illness" was previous published in *Rattle*.

**Margo Berdeshevsky**, NYC born, addicted to café au lait, writes in Paris. Her books: *Before The Drought*, finalist for National Poetry Series (Glass Lyre Press, 2017), *Between Soul & Stone, But a Passage in Wilderness*, (Sheep Meadow Press), *Beautiful Soon Enough*, first Ronald Sukenick Innovative Fiction Award (FC2). Honors: Robert H. Winner Award. Contributor to *Poetry International*, *New Letters*, *Kenyon Review*, *Plume*, *The Collagist*, *Gulf Coast*, *Southern Humanities Review*, *The American Journal of Poetry*. http://margoberdeshevsky.com

**Adria Bernardi** has authored a collection of essays, *Dead Meander*, and two novels, *Openwork*, and *The Day Laid on the Altar* (awarded the Bakeless Prize). Her short story collection *In the Gathering Woods* was awarded the 2000 Drue Heinz Literature Prize by Frank Conroy. She has taught fiction-writing at the Warren Wilson MFA and at Clark University. She lives in Nashville, where she now strives to drink coffee only in the morning, in search of good sleep and the limiting of migraine. adriabernardi.com

**Jane Blanchard** lives with serious consumers of coffee in Georgia. Her poetry has been published around the world as well as posted online. Her collections are *Unloosed* and *Tides & Currents*, both available from Kelsay Books.

"New Brew of Coffee" was previously published in *Halcyon*.

**Janet Bowdan**'s poems have appeared in *APR*, *Best American Poetry 2000*, *Blood Orange Review*, *Peacock Journal*, *Tahoma Literary Review*, and elsewhere; her chapbook, *Making Progress*, can be found at FinishingLinePress.com. She lives in Northampton, Massachusetts, with her husband, son, and sometimes a lovely stepdaughter or two. If she has no milk, she will stir a little ice cream into her coffee.

**Chanel Brenner** is author of *Vanilla Milk: a memoir told in poems*, (Silver Birch Press, 2014), a finalist for the Independent Book Award (2016). Her poems have appeared in *New Ohio Review*, *Poet Lore*, *Rattle*, *Muzzle Magazine*, *Pittsburgh Poetry Review*, *Barrow Street*, *Salamander*, and others. She adds, "I stopped drinking coffee when I was trying to get pregnant with my first child and abstained for seven years. When I started again, I realized how much I missed it. *What was I thinking?*"

"Something Has Lifted" was previously published in *West Trestle Review*, February 2015.

"To the Frustrated Mother at Starbucks with her Three-year-old Son" was previously published in *Rattle*, May 2016.

**Shirley J. Brewer** graduated from careers in bartending and speech therapy. She serves as poet-in-residence at Carver Center for the Arts in Baltimore, MD. Her poems garnish *Barrow Street*, *Poetry East*, *Slant*, *Gargoyle*, *Comstock Review*, among many others. Shirley's poetry books include *A Little Breast Music*, (Passager Books, 2008), *After Words* (Apprentice House, 2013), and *Bistro in Another Realm* (Main Street Rag, 2017). She has spilled coffee on numerous books and most of her clothes.

Poet and critic **Joel Brouwer** is the author of the collections *Exactly What Happened*, *Centuries*, *And So*, and *Off Message*. His poems, essays, and reviews have appeared in *Boston Review*, *Crazyhorse*, *New York Times Book Review*, *Paris Review*, *Ploughshares*, *Poetry*, *Tin House*, *Washington Post Book World*, and other publications. He has held fellowships from the National Endowment for the Arts, the Mrs. Giles Whiting Foundation, and the John Simon Guggenheim Foundation. He is chair of the Department of English at the University of Alabama.

"Coffee and Oranges" first appeared in *Poetry* (2005).

**Jeanne Bryner** is from Appalachia, land of sweet tea, but as a retired ER nurse, she knows the taste of coffee in its many stages of decline. And while it has been a comfort on midnights, she loved it most (blonde and sweet) over homemade bread in her mother's kitchen before any door opened taking them to another realm. She'd trade all her books and awards for a long, lazy morning with her mom.

"Rain" was previously published in *Journal of Emergency Nursing*, Volume 20, Number 3, June 1994.

"The Bread of Longing" appeared in her book *No Matter How Many Windows* (Wind Publications).

232

**Jeff Burt** lives in California with his wife amid the redwoods and two-lane roads wide enough for one car. A favorite date with his wife necessitates Turkish coffee ice cream. He has work in *The Watershed Review*, *The Nervous Breakdown*, *Spry*, *Atticus Review*, and *The Monarch Review*. He was the featured 2015 summer issue poet of *Clerestory* and won the 2017 *Cold Mountain Review* narrative poetry prize.

**Matthew Byrne** earned an MFA in poetry from University of Montana. His poem "Let Me Count the Ways" was featured in *The Best American Poetry 2007*, and his chapbook, *Silent Partner*, won the 2013 Sow's Ear Press Chapbook Award. If coffee didn't dehydrate the body, stink up the breath, skyrocket the blood pressure, induce trigger-happy mania, and cost so damn much, Matthew would have it strapped to his back all day and night with a straw, courtesy of his woefully neglected Camelbak.

**Jennifer Campbell** is an English professor in Buffalo, NY, and a co-editor of *Earth's Daughters*. She has two collections of poetry, *Supposed to Love* and *Driving Straight Through*. Recent work appears in *Pinyon Review*, *The Healing Muse*, *Xanadu*, *Comstock*, *Common Ground Review*, *Saranac Review*, and *Sow's Ear*. Coffee is often the last thing Jennifer thinks about at night and the first thing she considers in the morning.

**Laura Cherry** is the author of the collection *Haunts* (Cooper Dillon Books) and the chapbooks *Two White Beds* (Minerva Rising) and *What We Planted* (Providence Athenaeum). She co-edited the anthology *Poem, Revised* (Marion Street Press). Her work has been published in journals including *Antiphon*, *Ekphrastic Review*, *Los Angeles Review*, *Cider Press Review*, and *Hartskill Review*. She's strictly a second-wave coffee drinker: French Roast all the way, opaquely black and boiling hot, or don't bother.

"Story for a Dull World" previously appeared in *Vocabula Review* and in *Haunts* (Cooper Dillon Books).

**Justin Chotikul** is a caffeine-operated writer, photographer, and bookseller in San Francisco.

**Kersten Christianson** is a raven-watching, moon-gazing Alaskan. When not exploring the summer lands and dark winter of the Yukon Territory, she resides in Sitka. She earned her MFA in Creative Writing through the University of Alaska Anchorage in 2016. Kersten's recent work has appeared in *Cirque*, *Tidal Echoes*, and *Sheila-Na-Gig*. Her poetry collection *Something Yet to Be Named* (Aldrich Press) was published in 2017. Kersten co-edits the quarterly journal *Alaska Women Speak*. Blog: www.kerstenchristianson.com

"Dutch Fry Baby" was previously published by *Ink Drift* (2016).

**Joan Colby** has 21 books, the latest, *Her Heartsongs* (Presa Press). Her *Selected Poems* won the 2013 FutureCycle Book Prize and *Ribcage* won the 2015 Kithara Book Prize. She starts every day with coffee, grinding fresh beans and making a pot in her Krups coffeemaker. She isn't wedded to any one brand, but tends to favor Peets, Starbucks, or Dunkin Donuts. She drinks it black and is vehemently opposed to defiling her coffee with substances such as milk, cream, or sugar. She has never had a latte.

"Black Coffee" was previously published in *Sing Heavenly Muse.*

**Jessica Cory** teaches in the English Department at Western Carolina University. She is the editor and a contributor to the forthcoming *Where the Sweet Waters Flow: Contemporary Appalachian Nature Writing* with West Virginia University Press. Her work has previously been published in *A Poetry Congeries, ellipsis…, Appalachian Heritage,* and other journals. She is an avid fan of Irish coffee with whipped cream.

**Linda M. Crate**'s works have been published in numerous magazines and anthologies both online and in print. She is the author of four published chapbooks, the latest of which is *My*

234

*Wings Were Made to Fly* (Flutter Press, September 2017). She has many relatives that enjoy coffee, but personally she finds the taste a little too bitter.

**Barbara Crooker** is the author of eight books of poetry; *Les Fauves* is the most recent. Her work has appeared in many anthologies, including *The Poetry of Presence* and *Nasty Women: An Unapologetic Anthology of Subversive Verse*, and she has received a number of awards, including the WB Yeats Society of New York Award, and the Thomas Merton Poetry of the Sacred Award. Life would not be worth living without French Roast coffee.

"How to Disappear" was first published in *The MacGuffin*.

**Deborah Crooks** is a writer and performing singer-songwriter living in Alameda, CA. She's released a number or records under her own name and with the band Bay Station. Previous publications include *No Depression, Kitchen Sink*, and in the anthology *The Thinking Girl's Guide to Enlightenment* (Seal Press). She currently drinks her coffee (organic, Fair Trade, medium/dark roast) black. www.deborahcrooks.com

**Isabella Cruz** is a Florida based writer whose works have previously appeared in *Wigleaf* and *The View*. Coffee is both the lifeblood and catalyst at the root of many of her pieces. She has confronted many a moment of heaving hysteria with a mug in her hand, only to end up becoming both the *schlemiel* and *schlimazel*.

**Kwame Dawes** has authored twenty-one books of poetry and numerous books of fiction, criticism, and essays. His most recent collection, *City of Bones: A Testament*, appeared in 2017. His awards include the Forward Poetry Prize, The Hollis Summers Poetry Prize, The Musgrave Silver Medal, several Pushcart Prizes, and an Emmy. He is Chancellor Professor of English at the University of Nebraska. Dawes serves as the Associate Poetry Editor for Peepal Tree Books and is Director of the African Poetry Book Fund. He is Series Editor of the African Poetry Book Series and Artistic Director of the Calabash International Literary Festival. In 2018, he was elected a Chancellor of the Academy of American Poets.

"Coffee Break" was first published in *Hope's Hospice* (Peepal Tree Press).

**Carol L. Deering** has twice received the Wyoming Arts Council Poetry Fellowship (2016 judge Rebecca Foust; 1999 judge Agha Shahid Ali). Her poetry appears in online and traditional journals and anthologies. She couldn't get through a morning without a good cup of coffee. In New England, where she was born and grew up, regular coffee included cream and sugar; but she has grown accustomed to the West (wilderness, a campfire), where regular coffee is black.

**Stephen Dobyns** has published forty-one books of poems, novels, short stories and essays. His most recent works are *The Day's Last Light Reddens the Leaves of the Copper Beech* (poems, BOA Editions, 2016) and *Saratoga Payback* (novel, Blue Rider/Penguin, 2017). Dobyns has mostly taught in the MFA Program of Warren Wilson College, and at more than half a dozen other universities. He adds, "Every morning for over fifty years I've drunk one or more cups of dark French Roast coffee brewed in a succession of Gaggia espresso machines. Though it would be wrong to say that those many thousand cups of French Roast made me what I am today, they have certainly helped."

"[Over a Cup of Coffee]" first appeared in *Poetry* (December, 2001). It later appears in his book of poems, aphorisms and definitions *The Porcupine's Kisses*, (Penguin Books, 2002).

**Patrick Donnelly** is the author of four books of poetry: *The Charge* (Ausable Press, 2003, since 2009 part of Copper Canyon Press), *Nocturnes of the Brothel of Ruin* (Four Way Books, 2012), *Jesus Said* (a chapbook from Orison Books, 2017), and *Little-Known Operas* (Four Way Books, 2019).

236

Donnelly is director of the Poetry Seminar at The Frost Place, a center for poetry and the arts, and in Italy, he orders a *latte macchiato con doppio*.

"Instant Coffee" was previously published in *The Charge* (Ausable Press, 2003, since 2009 part of Copper Canyon Press), and before that, in *The Yale Review*.

**Barbara Drake** is a retired Linfield College professor, grandmother, and author of *Driving One Hundred*, *Peace at Heart*, *Morning Light*, *Writing Poetry*, and other works. She and her husband live in Oregon's rural Yamhill County. Every morning before walking their border collies she makes a strong pot of espresso in her well-used Bialetti and sips it slowly while gazing west toward the Oregon Coast Range and wondering what the day will bring.

"Milky Coffee" was previously published in *Windfall* magazine, Fall 2010, Portland, Oregon.

**Lois Parker Edstrom**, a retired nurse, is the author of four collections of poetry. Her poems have been read by Garrison Keillor on *The Writer's Almanac*, featured by Ted Kooser in *American Life in Poetry*, adapted to dance, and transcribed into Braille. Edstrom's poems have appeared in numerous literary journals. She married into a Swedish family of committed coffee drinkers and lives with her husband on an island off the coast of Washington.

"Last Days" and "Small Town Coffee House" appear in *Glint* (MoonPath Press, 2019).

**Martín Espada**'s many books of poems include *Vivas to Those Who Have Failed* (2016), *The Trouble Ball* (2011), *The Republic of Poetry* (2006) and *Alabanza* (2003). He has received the Ruth Lilly Poetry Prize, the Shelley Memorial Award, an Academy of American Poets Fellowship, and a Guggenheim Fellowship. He is a professor of English at the University of Massachusetts-Amherst. He does not drink coffee, which would deeply offend his grandmother.

"Preciosa Like a Last Cup of Coffee" appears in *A Mayan Astronomer in Hell's Kitchen* (W. W. Norton & Company, 2001).

**Jean Esteve** takes her coffee with hot milk; her poetry with a grain of salt.

**Dina Ripsman Eylon** is the founder of the Vaughan Poets' Circle. Her English and Hebrew poems were published in literary magazines, journals, and anthologies. Her latest books are *In the Heart of the City and Other Urban Poems*, available at sisterhoodpress.com, *On the Horizon in the First Person* [Hebrew], *Songs of Love and Misgivings* (2nd edition), and the bilingual collection, *Until Borders Collapse*. She can only start her day after the coffee kicks in.

**Alexis Rhone Fancher**'s a fool for French Roast, her poems fueled by caffeine. She is published in *Best American Poetry 2016*, *Verse Daily*, *Plume*, *Rattle*, *Rust + Moth*, *The MacGuffin*, *Anomaly Lit Review*, *Diode*, *The American Journal of Poetry*, and elsewhere. She's the author of four poetry collections, most recently *Enter Here* (2017), and *Junkie Wife* (2018). A multiple Pushcart Prize and Best of the Net nominee, Alexis is poetry editor of *Cultural Weekly*. www.alexisrhonefancher.com

"For the Sad Waitress at the Diner in Barstow" was published in *The San Pedro River Review* in 2016, and also on line at *Verse Daily* in 2017.

**Kristin Fast** hails from central Alberta, where she explores the mountains and the prairies with her husband and two dogs. Her writing plays with mythologies and fairy tales, early modern and modernist styles, and a healthy dose of sensory detail. Coffee is a love she was slow to embrace—except when paired with chocolate cake!—but now she's a dogged pursuer of the perfectly pulled espresso shot.

Former librarian **Krystyna Fedosejevs** writes poetry, flash fiction, and short stories. Coffee's a must. It should entice with exotic aroma and rich flavor, flow through her veins all day long. Krystyna is published in Canada, United States, and Europe in journals, anthologies, and online including *Boston Literary Magazine* and *Friday Flash Fiction*. She won several poetry contests, was shortlisted in a short story competition, and is a member of two writers' groups where she resides.

**Paul Fisher**'s wife once worked for Starbucks in their original small roastery. Visual artist as well as poet, he earned an MFA in Poetry from New England College. His first book, *Rumors of Shore*, was published in 2010, his second, *An Exaltation of Tongues*, in 2017. Paul's poems have appeared in many venues, including *The Antioch Review, Cave Wall, Crab Creek Review, Cutthroat, Innisfree Poetry Journal, Nimrod*, and *Switched-on Gutenberg*.

Albuquerque writer **Mark Fleisher** has published three collections, most recently *Reflections: Soundings from the Deep*, a compilation of poetry, prose, and photographs. His work has appeared in several anthologies, in print and on line. Fleisher earned a journalism degree from Ohio University. His Air Force service included a year as a combat news reporter in Vietnam. Two cups of ultra-strong Vietnamese coffee get his creative juices flowing each morning.

"Ask Albert" appears in *Reflections: Soundings from the Deep* (Mercury HeartLink, 2018).

**Laura Foley** has authored six poetry collections. Her poem "Gratitude List" won the Common Good Books contest and was featured on *The Writer's Almanac*. "Nine Ways" won the Outermost Poetry Contest, judged by Marge Piercy. A hospice volunteer, she lives with her wife among Vermont hills, where her love-relationship to coffee, especially cappuccino, knows no bounds. Her daughter once observed: "Mom, you know all the best coffee shops along the East Coast!"—a sentiment with which Laura humbly concurs.

"My Own Hand" was first published in *Night Ringing* (Headmistress Press).

**Gina Forberg** recently obtained her MFA from Manhattanville College. Her chapbook *Leaving Normal* was published in 2017 from Finishing Line Press. Her relationship with coffee began after college when she would start falling asleep at her desk around three in the afternoon. It started off light and sweet, but now she prefers dark roast with a shot of espresso and light cream. She lives in Fairfield Connecticut with her family.

**Jennifer L. Freed** writes, teaches, and raises her daughters in Massachusetts. Her recent poetry appears or is forthcoming in journals including *Atlanta Review, Zone 3, Connecticut River Review, The Worcester Review,* and *Amsterdam Quarterly,* and has twice been nominated for a Pushcart Prize. Her chapbook, *These Hands Still Holding,* was a finalist for the 2013 New Woman's Voices prize. She started drinking coffee when she was teaching English in Prague in 1996.

**Kenneth Fries** writes: Start the day with a cup of java, inhale the steam, stare deep into the swirling black. Think abyss. Think taste. Taste the abyss of the day. Also, the flavor. Find flavor stimulating, let it in, let it lead to something. Blueberry pancakes? Maybe. Or write something new, fresh, in accord with sunrise. The world is always turning toward the morning. There are fewer of them now, but birds still sing. With clear bell song in the blue dawn. With relentless courage. Put that in the pen. Try the line, maybe, something like "Who will open the green door of my heart? Will it be you?"

**Joshua Gage** is an ornery curmudgeon from Cleveland. He is the author of five collections of poetry. His newest chapbook,

*Necromancy*, is available on Locofo Chaps from Moria Press. He is a graduate of the Low Residency MFA Program in Creative Writing at Naropa University. He has a penchant for Pendleton shirts and any poem strong enough to yank the breath out of his lungs.

**Myrna Garanis** was too young to imbibe, but loved the aroma emanating from the green coffee grinder attached to her Norwegian grandparents' kitchen wall. Freshly ground coffee still conjures up mornings spent in that farm home. Myrna lives in Edmonton, Alberta. Her essay/poem collection *All Tied Up* is currently hunting for a coffee-friendly home.

**David Giannini**'s most recent poetry collections include *The Future Only Rattles When You Pick It Up* and *Faces Somewhere Wild* (Dos Madres Press, 2017, 2018); *Four Plus Four* (Country Valley Press, 2017); and *Porous Borders* (Spuyten Duyvil Press, 2017). His work appears in national and international literary magazines and anthologies, including *New Hungers for Old: One-Hundred Years of Italian-American Poetry*. He was nominated for a Pushcart Prize in 2015. Coffee is the mother of invention!

"Mug Shot" appeared in Giannini's book of prose poems *Porous Borders* (Spuyten Duyvil Press, 2017).

**Tzivia Gover** is the author of several books, including *The Mindful Way to a Good Night's Sleep*. Her poetry has been published widely in periodicals, journals, and anthologies. She combines her love of dreams and poetry by teaching writing workshops that bring these two creative processes together. She received her MFA in writing from Columbia University. A recovering picky eater, she had her first cup of coffee at age 53. For more information visit www.tziviagover.com.

**Anne Graue**, the author of *Fig Tree in Winter* (Dancing Girl Press), has published poems in anthologies and literary journals, online and in print. She is a contributing editor for the Saturday Poetry Series at Asitoughttobe.com and has been a reviewer for *NewPages.com* and the *Margaret Atwood Society Journal*. She enjoys fair-trade dark roast with a bit of cream in her New York home.

"Drinking Coffee in Occupied Cyprus" was published in *Squalorly Literary Journal*, Summer 2015.

**Larkin Edwin Greer** was previously a trial lawyer, prosecuting and later defending federal criminal cases. He now writes fiction and poetry full time. His novels and poems have been finalists several times in creative writing contests, and he's had poetry published in *Blueline* and as an Editor's Pick in *Pooled Ink*. He claims that the fabled muse is a pool of deep black java steaming in a time-honored mug.

**John Grey** is an Australian poet, US resident. Recently published in *Examined Life Journal*, *Studio One*, and *Columbia Review*, with work upcoming in *Leading Edge*, *Poetry East*, and *Midwest Quarterly*.

**Gwen Gunn** has had poems published in *Connecticut Poets at Work*, *The Guilford Anthology*, *Connecticut River Review*, *Fresh Ink*, and *Caduceus*. She co-edited the poetry magazine *Embers*, and with the Guilford Poets Guild helps to organize the Second Thursday Poetry Series in Guilford, Connecticut. Her poetry and painting chapbook, *Tastes*, was recently published. Since a trip to Eugene, Oregon, she has desired a good strong espresso every afternoon at her favorite local cafe, Cilantros.

When **Tom Hansen** was ten, his German grandmother made him his first cup of coffee—heavy on the milk and sugar. That was the beginning of a lifelong love affair. His poems have appeared in *The Literary Review*, *The Midwest Quarterly*, *The Paris Review*, *Weber: The Contemporary West*, and others. His book, *Falling to Earth*, winner of the A. Poulin, Jr. Poetry Prize, was published by BOA Editions.

**Anna Harris-Parker**'s poems have appeared or are forthcoming in *Cellpoems, Poetry for the Masses, Mikrokosmos, SLANT*, and *West Texas Literary Review*. She teaches at Augusta University, and lives in Georgia with her husband and their two dogs. She enjoys drinking coffee (with a little cream) while watching the backyard birds outside of the bay window in her kitchen.

**Preeti Hay** is a published freelance writer. She loves to write fiction, personal essays, and sometimes gets lucky with poetry. Her love for coffee started young when she started to sneak instant coffee into her daily glass of milk. Her teenage years were spent exploring the world of coffee and daydreaming of being a barista while wanting to build a spaceship to escape, in case planet earth stops growing coffee.

**Ilona Hegedus** is a Hungarian writer who lives in Budapest, Hungary. Her poems have appeared in the US, UK, Greece, and Hungary; amongst many others in *Tales of The Talisman* magazine, *Illumen*, and *Universe Pathways*. She is a graduate with a degree in English and she started to drink coffee when she was still a student. Her blog: http://ilonasworld.blogspot.hu

**Grey Held** is a recipient of a NEA Fellowship in Creative Writing. He's published two poetry collections, *Two-Star General* (Brick Road Poetry Press, 2012) and *Spilled Milk* (Word Press, 2013). He works closely with the Mayor's Office of Cultural Affairs in Newton, MA to direct projects that connect contemporary poets (and their poetry) with a wider audience. For his morning brew, Grey grinds his own coffee beans and prefers the pour-over method for its slow watchful pleasure.

**Diane Henningfeld** grew up in Howland Corners, Ohio, and began drinking coffee while working at her father's hardware store. Her work has appeared in *Storm Cellar, Dunes Review, The Michigan Poet, Penwood Review, Flash Fiction Magazine,*

243

and in her chapbook *Turning* (2015). She also has authored/ edited over 25 nonfiction books for young adults. She lives with her husband in Adrian, Michigan, where she taught literature at Adrian College for over twenty years.

**Ed Higgins'** poems and short fiction have appeared in various print and online journals including recently: *Peacock Journal, Uut Poetry, Triggerfish Critical Review, and Tigershark Magazine,* among others. Ed teaches literature at George Fox University, south of Portland, OR. and is Asst. Fiction Editor for Ireland-based *Brilliant Flash Fiction.* As for coffee he says, he never drinks water unless it has coffee in it.

"Over Lattés" appears in *The Coffee Press Journal,* 2005.

**David D. Horowitz** founded and manages Rose Alley Press, which published his latest collection, *Cathedral and Highrise.* David's poems have appeared in many journals and anthologies, including *Candelabrum, The New Formalist, Terrain.org, Raven Chronicles, The Lyric,* and *Here, There, and Everywhere,* and his essays regularly appear in *Exterminating Angel.* He frequently organizes readings in and around Seattle. For over sixteen years as a law firm conference room attendant, David serviced many coffee machines.

"Friday Evening's Fifty Stories" appeared in *Cathedral and Highrise* (Rose Alley Press, 2015).

"Place" appeared in *Sky Above the Temple* (Rose Alley Press, 2012).

**M.J. Iuppa's** fourth poetry collection is *This Thirst* (Kelsay Books, 2017). For the past 29 years, she has lived on a small farm near the shores of Lake Ontario. She says: *Coffee can be bittersweet.* Check out her blog: mjiuppa.blogspot.com for her musings on writing, sustainability & life's stew.

**Adiba Jaigirdar** is an Irish/Bangladeshi writer and poet. She resides in Dublin, Ireland and has an MA in postcolonal studies. Her work has been published in *200ccs*, *About Place Journal*, and many others. She works as an ESL teacher, and occasionally writes about pop culture for *Cultured Vultures* and books for *Bookriot*. She is the co-founder and editor of *Spectra*, an online feminist publication. All of her work is aided by copious amounts of coffee.

**D. R. James** has taught writing, literature, and peace-making at Hope College for 33 years and lives outside Saugatuck, Michigan. Recent collections include *If god were gentle* (Dos Madres), *Split-Level*, and *Why War* (both Finishing Line). When not cycling with his wife, psychotherapist Suzy Doyle, he divides his free time between staring at the woods from a recliner and staring at the woods from a deck chair, a mug of Love Buzz always at hand.

"Love Buzz" was first published in *Peacock Journal*, November 2017.

"Reassurance to My Future Spouse" was first published in *A Little Instability without Birds* (Finishing Line Press, 2006).

**Mitch James** has three degrees, one terminal, in various fields of English studies. He's had fiction, poetry, and scholarship on creative writing and composition studies published in a handful of venues, most of which can be found here: mitchjamesauthor.com. He writes in the wee hours of the morning, sipping his first cup of coffee during the same time he used to slug back his last whiskey. He calls it adulthood.

"McDonalds, Indiana, PA. January 2009" was previously published in *I Speak the Password Primeval 1*, June 2009.

**Dale Jensen** was born in Oakland, California, and has degrees in psychology from UC Berkeley and the University of Toronto. He has seven books and three chapbooks out, and edited the poetry magazine *Malthus*. He lives in Berkeley, California, with his wife, the poet Judy Wells. He grew up in a Scandinavian-American household in which coffee was just short of a sacrament and retains that love of coffee (and coffeehouses) to this day.

"Fast as a New York Sonnet" originally appeared in *Yew Nork* (2014).

**Jeffrey Johannes** is an artist and poet whose work has been published in journals, including *Modern Haiku, Rosebud, Nimrod,* and *Wisconsin Academy Review*. He co-edited the 2012 *WI Poets' Calendar*. On his Facebook page, Jeffrey posts *Coffee Companions*, which is art work he enjoys looking at while drinking his morning coffee. He lives in Port Edwards, WI with his poet wife, Joan.

"Silence" was previously published in the *2003 Wisconsin Fellowship of Poets' Calendar* and on the *Your Daily Poem* website.

"Visitation" was previously published in his chapbook *Ritual for Beginning Again*.

Following a career as a U.S. Army musician, **Gordon Kippola** earned an MFA in Creative Writing at the University of Tampa. This poem was fueled by approximately 25 mugs (yes, THAT mug!) of Folgers Black Silk coffee (brewed with a responsibly reusable plastic Keurigy-thingy), and inspired by a prompt from Kim Addonizio during her online workshop. The author thanks Kim and his fellow poets for their helpful suggestions.

**Karen Klassen** was raised in Vancouver, BC by her Mennonite immigrant parents. Much of her writing has been inspired by her childhood and upbringing. Her work can be found in numerous journals and has also been read on CBC radio. Karen loves beachy holidays, puttering in the garden and piping hot lattes. She currently lives in Kamloops, BC.

**Stephen J. Kudless** is a widely published poet and playwright. Two of his plays (*Beds* and *How Fish Breathe*) have been staged in off-off-Broadway venues. His poems have appeared in *Mona Poetica, The Poetry Project, Inverso* (Italy), *Freefall* (Canada), *The New York Times*, and many other publications. His poem "The Color Hazel" won the Lawrence Durrell White Mice Competition (2015). He lives in New York City, and starts every day with two cups of Arabica, iced in the summer, and hot in the winter.

**Angel Latterell** originates from Duluth, Minnesota and currently resides in Seattle, Washington where she works as an attorney, project manager, and teacher of mindfulness and empowerment. On most days she drinks dark roast coffee from a French press; on odd days it's flavored coffee from a Keurig machine. Her poems have appeared in *About Place, Fault Lines, Clare,* and *Colere,* and her theater production *Intersection: a spoken word opera* debuted at Hugo House in Seattle in 2007.

**Dorianne Laux**'s fifth collection, *The Book of Men,* was awarded The Paterson Prize. Her fourth book of poems, *Facts About the Moon* won The Oregon Book Award. Her collection *What We Carry* was a finalist for the National Book Critic's Circle Award. She is the co-author of the celebrated text *The Poet's Companion: A Guide to the Pleasures of Writing Poetry.* Laux teaches poetry in the Program in Creative Writing at North Carolina State University and is a founding faculty member of Pacific University's Low Residency MFA Program. Her latest collection is *Only As the Day Is Long: New and Selected* (W.W. Norton, 2019).

"Bird" first appeared in *Awake,* (Carnegie Mellon Univ. Press, 1990).

**Ron. Lavalette** lives in Vermont. He can't remember what coffee tastes like without a glug or two of Kahlua. His work has appeared extensively in journals, reviews, and anthologies ranging alphabetically from *Able Muse* and the *Anthology of New England Poets* through the *World Haiku Review* and

*Your One Phone Call.* A reasonable sample of his published work can be viewed at: http://eggsovertokyo.blogspot.com

A retired science writer-editor, **Dee LeRoy** lives in Maryland, where she once spent time at a now out-of-business Caffe Appassionato. She finds that places where coffee is brewing seem friendly and that a cup of good coffee can enrich moments alone as well as those spent with others. Dee's poems have appeared in numerous literary magazines. Her first poetry collection, *Earthbound,* was named to *Kirkus Reviews'* Best books of 2015.

**Lori Levy**'s poems have appeared in numerous literary journals and anthologies in the U.S., England, and Israel. One of her poems was read on a program on BBC Radio 4. She lives with her family in Los Angeles, but "home" has also been Vermont and Israel. Lori begins her day with coffee and toast and is addicted to her coffee and cookies ritual every day.

"Lukewarm" was published previously in the Spring 2014 issue of *The Broad River Review.*

**Ellaraine Lockie** is widely published and awarded as a poet, nonfiction book author, and essayist. She also teaches writing workshops and serves as Poetry Editor for the lifestyles magazine, *Lilipoh.* She writes every morning in a coffee shop no matter where she is. One of her thirteen chapbooks is entitled *Coffee House Confessions* and consists of poems written in and about coffee shops around the world.

"In the Privacy of Public" was first published in *Taproot Literary Review.*

**Joel Long**'s book *Winged Insects* won the White Pine Press Poetry Prize. *Lessons in Disappearance* and *Knowing Time by Light* were published by Blaine Creek Press in 2010. His chapbooks, *Chopin's Preludes* and *Saffron Beneath Every Frost* were published from Elik Press. He lives in Salt Lake City.

**Sharon MacFarlane** writes both prose and poetry. She lives in rural Saskatchewan and goes to coffee row at the local café every Tuesday morning.

**Katharyn Howd Machan** had her first cup of coffee in 1970 when she was 17 at a weak-fooded banquet while at a competition for the performance of literature. She went on to write a dissertation years later for Northwestern University called *The Writer as Performer*. A professor of Writing at Ithaca College, she has authored 38 published collections of poems, most recently *What the Piper Promised*, winner of the *New Alexandria Quarterly* chapbook competition.

"French Coffee" first appeared in *Pinyon*, No. 27 (Spring 2018).

"Friday, Coffee" first appeared in *ByLine* (March 1998).

**Roy Mash** is the author of *Buyer's Remorse* (Cherry Grove, 2014). Following retirement, coffee stepped in to fill the vacuum. On any given afternoon you may find him staring out of a cafe window, dabbing up the seeds that have fallen from an everything bagel, and mentally thumbing over his poems that have appeared widely in journals such as: *AGNI Online, Barrow Street, The Evansville Review, Passages North, Poetry East, RHINO,* and *River Styx.*

"The Plagiarizer of Words" first appeared in *Larkfield Review*, and was reprinted in *Buyer's Remorse* (Cherry Grove, 2014).

**Pat McCutcheon** taught English for thirty years at College of the Redwoods, where she loved students and teaching creative writing, and hated department meetings and grading papers. Her first chapbook was *Recovering Perfectionist*, and in 2015 a second, *Slipped Past Words*, was a winner in Finishing Line Press's Chapbook contest. Braced by strong French Roast of a morning, Pat begins to percolate.

**Deborah Meltvedt** is a writer and Medical Science teacher in Sacramento, California. Deborah has been published in the *American River Literary Review, Under the Gum Tree, SPC Tule Review, Susurrus,* and *Creative Non-Fiction Anthology.* Deborah began drinking coffee at age thirteen as a bonding ritual with her mother. Back then lots of sugar. Now she takes her coffee black and enjoys it every morning next to her husband Rick and their cat, Anchovy Jack.

**Joseph Millar**'s first collection, *Overtime,* was a finalist for the 2001 Oregon Book Award. His latest collection is *Kingdom* (2017). Millar grew up in Pennsylvania, attended Johns Hopkins University, and spent 30 years in the Bay area working at a variety of jobs from telephone repairman to commercial fisherman. He has won fellowships from the Guggenheim Foundation and the National Endowment for the Arts, as well as a Pushcart Prize. Millar teaches in Pacific University's low-residency MFA Program and in North Carolina State's MFA Program in Creative Writing.

"The Day After Sinatra Married Mia Farrow" previously appeared *New Letters.*

In addition to writing poetry, **Ilene Millman** is a speech/language pathologist with many years' experience teaching literacy skills to children who learn differently. She lives in New Jersey. Her poems have appeared in journals including *Paterson Review, PoemMemoirStory, The Sow's Ear,* and others. Her first collection, *Adjust Speed to Weather,* was published in 2017. She adds, "my morning cup of coffee is a given, but for too many, nothing is to be taken for granted."

"Bars, Beggars" previously appeared in *Adjust Speed to Weather* (PrintPod Publications, 2017).

A 2018 Jack Straw Writer, **Natasha Kochicheril Moni**'s publication credits include *Magma, The Rumpus, Entropy,* one full-length poetry collection (*The Cardiologist's Daughter,*

Two Sylvias Press, 2014) and two poetry chapbook collections (*Lay Down Your Fleece*, Shirt Pocket Press, 2017 and *Nearly* (Dancing Girl Press, 2018). Natasha's optimism increases exponentially, after her first sip of coffee.

"We Have Been Here Before" was first published in Brightly Press' *Shake The Tree* anthology.

**Robin Amelia Morris** grew up in New Jersey, in a family that collected books and cats, both of which she continues to gather around her, though she has succeeded in leaving behind the instant coffee granules her mother stirred into boiling water each morning; instead, Morris brews potfuls of Big Bang and drinks this coffee in Western Massachusetts where, as an online professor, she teaches students who reside around the world.

**Meryl Natchez's** most recent book is a bilingual volume of translations: *Poems From the Stray Dog Café: Akhmatova, Mandelstam and Gumilev*. Her work has appeared in *The American Journal of Poetry, ZYZZYVA, Rappahannock Review, Pinch Literary Review, Atlanta Review, Lyric, The Moth, Comstock Review*, and has won various awards. She is on the board of Marin Poetry Center and blogs at www.dactyls-and-drakes.com. She avers that without coffee, many of these poems would not exist.

"Poem for Paul" previously received an Award of Merit and was published by *Comstock Review*.

**Patricia Horn O'Brien** is a member of the Guilford Poetry Guild and recently co-founded CT River Poets. She's facilitated poetry workshops, including at York C.I. hospice program and Middlesex Community College. Pat's been published in various periodicals, including *Poet Lore, Caduceus*, and *Freshwater*. Her many prizes include: Trumbull Arts Counsel, Embers, and the National Federation of State Poetry Societies. She recently published her first book of poetry, *When Less Than Perfect is Enough*.

**Korkut Onaran** is author of *The Trident Poems* (World Enough Writers, 2018) and *The Book of Colors* (Cervena Barva Press Chapbook Award, 2007). His poetry has been published in journals such as *Penumbra, Rhino, Water~Stone, Review, Atlanta Review, Common Ground Review,* and *Baltimore Review.* Korkut owns an urban planning and architecture firm in Boulder, Colorado and teaches at the University of Colorado at Denver. Originally from Turkey, he lives with his wife Jennifer B. Frank in Longmont, Colorado. Though he writes at local coffee houses, he drinks tea.

"A December Sunrise" first appeared in *The Trident Poems* (World Enough Writers, 2018).

**Rachel Tepfer Orzoff** is a real New Yorker from suburban Chicago who lives in Minneapolis. She spends her time dangling participles, capping toothpaste tubes, and other single-mom mundanities. Both in her dreams and her leisure she is an alto chanteuse (though in the dreams she gets paid for it). Sadly, until further notice, she is not allowed to drink coffee! Seems to make her world a lot less vivid, though surprisingly, just as fast.

"Growing Up One Cup at a Time" was originally published under the title "Coffee" in *East on Central*, Volume 10 (2011-2012).

**Keli Osborn** works with community organizations and drinks hot, black coffee dripped through an unbleached filter in a red cone. Her poems appear in *Confrontation Literary Magazine, The Fourth River,* and *Timberline Review,* and anthologies including *The Donut Book* and *Nasty Women Poets: An Unapologetic Anthology of Subversive Verse.* Keli won Ooligan Press's Write to Publish 2016 Pacific Northwest Poetry Contest for her poem, "Blue Marble." She lives in Eugene, Oregon.

"Redwoods Diner" was first was published in *San Pedro River Review*, Vol. 9, No. 1, Spring 2017.

Poet, critic, and activist **Alicia Ostriker** was born in 1937 in New York City. She earned degrees from Brandeis and the University of Wisconsin-Madison. Twice a finalist for the National Book Award, Ostriker has published numerous volumes of poetry, including *Waiting for the Light* (2017), which was awarded the Berru Award from the Jewish Book Council, *The Old Woman, the Tulip, and the Dog* (2014), *The Book of Seventy* (2009), which received the Jewish National Book Award, *The Crack in Everything* (1996), which won the Paterson Award and the San Francisco State Poetry Center Award, and *The Imaginary Lover* (1986), which received the William Carlos Williams Award.

"Berkely: Youth and Age" appears in *The Crack in Everything* (University of Pittsburgh Press, 1996).

"Waiting for the Light" appears in *Waiting for the Light* (University of Pittsburgh Press, 2017).

Connecticut writer **Jen Payne** is inspired by those moments that move us most—love and loss, joy and disappointment, milestones and turning points. She prefers to write in the quiet of the morning, usually before 4 and always with coffee. She has published two books (*LOOK UP! Musings on the Nature of Mindfulness* and *Evidence of Flossing: What We Leave Behind*) and is a member of the Guilford Poets Guild. For more, please visit: www.randomactsofwriting.net.

**Francesca Pellegrino**'s publications include *Tutte le lucciole vennero al pettine, Chernobylove—il giorno dopo il vento, Dimentico sempre di dare l'acqua ai sogni,* and *Niente di personale.* In 2009, she was a finalist for the Turoldo poetry prize. Translations of her poems have appeared in *Asymptote, Cerise Press, Gradiva International Journal of Italian Literature, Journal of Italian Translation, Metamorphoses, Inventory,* and *Rhino.* Recent poems, including others in which the theme of coffee surfaces, can be found at her website: http://francescapellegrino.altervista.org/

"Café Correto With Vinavil," "Mokafury," and "Repeat Until," translated by Adria Bernardi, were published in Chernobylove—*The Day After the Wind, Selected Poems* (Chelsea Editions, 2014).

**George Perreault** has served as a visiting writer in New Mexico, Montana, and Utah, and his work has been nominated both for the Pushcart Prize and Best of the Net. Recent work appears in *The American Journal of Poetry; High Desert Journal; Timberline Review;* and *Weber—The Contemporary West.* "The best of my friends enjoy coffee deeply, and my avoidance is not principled, merely habitual— and probably a sign of bad character."

**LeeAnn Pickrell** lives in Richmond, California, where she works as a freelance editor and writes poetry and prose, often inspired by that first cup of coffee in the morning or by that afternoon nap followed by a cup of coffee. She prefers strong coffee softened only slightly by frothed soy milk. Her work recently appeared in *Eclectica Magazine's* anthology of best poetry and in *A Trembling of Finches.*

**Robert M. Randolph** teaches at Waynesburg University. He has been a Fulbright Scholar in Finland and Greece, and has published poems in about 50 journals in the USA and abroad. He likes poetry, the blues, and strong coffee. About "Cup of Blues," he says, "The coffee in that cup is strong enough to hold the past, the present, and the future."

**Donna Reis** is author of the poetry collection *No Passing Zone* (Deerbrook Editions, 2012) and non-fiction book *Seeking Ghosts in the Warwick Valley* (Schiffer Publishing, Ltd, 2003). She is co-editor and contributor to the anthology, *Blues for Bill: A Tribute to William Matthews* (Akron Poetry Series, 2005). During difficult times, she learned how getting together for a cup of coffee with friends created a safe haven to say what they would never utter elsewhere. *Hail Coffee!*

254

"Going for Coffee After an Al-Anon Meeting" previously appeared in *Snake Nation Review*.

**Jack Ridl**'s *Practicing to Walk Like a Heron* received the ForeWords Review Gold Medal for poetry. *Broken Symmetry* was named the year's best book of poetry by The Society of Midland Authors. Billy Collins chose his *Against Elegies* for the NYC Center for Book Arts Award. The Carnegie Foundation named him Michigan's Professor of the Year. More than 85 of his students are publishing.

"Morning in Key West" appears in *San Pedro Review*, 2017.

"Morning Rounds" was first published in *The Louisville Review*, and was subsequently published in *Practicing to Walk Like a Heron* (Wayne State University Press, 2013).

**Laura Ring**'s poetry has appeared or is forthcoming in *Lunch Ticket*, *Rise Up Review*, and *Rogue Agent*, among other places. A native Vermonter, she lives and works in Chicago. Laura is serious about caffeinated beverages. The first time she went camping, she packed her electric coffeemaker. She would also gladly travel ten thousand miles to drink South Indian filter coffee from a stainless steel tumbler.

**Alberto Álvaro Ríos** is the author of *The Theater of the Night* (Copper Canyon Press, 2016) and numerous other poetry collections, including *Whispering to Fool the Wind* (Sheep Meadow Press, 1982), which won the 1981 Walt Whitman Award, selected by Donald Justice. Other awards include six Pushcart Prizes in both poetry and fiction, the Arizona Governor's Arts Award, and fellowships from the Guggenheim Foundation and the National Endowment for the Arts. He is Regents Professor of English at Arizona State University in Tempe, where he has taught since 1982. In 2013, Ríos was named the inaugural state poet laureate of Arizona. In 2014, Ríos was elected a Chancellor of the Academy of American Poets.

"Coffee in the Afternoon" appeared in the *Atlanta Review* (Volume VII, Number 1. Fall / Winter 2000).

**James Miller Robinson** has authored two chapbooks: *The Caterpillars at Saint Bernard* (Mule on a Ferris Wheel Press) and *Boca del Río in the Afternoon* (Finishing Line Press). He is a legal/court interpreter of Spanish in Alabama. He adds, "I can't start the day without some time in solitude with my notebook and a cup of coffee. Both poems are set in Mexico City where I love to write in quaint cafés and in the early-morning quiet of in-laws' homes."

"Cafés Chinos" first appeared in *Snake Nation Review*, Issue 31.

**James Rodgers** is a prolific poet living in Pacific, WA for more than two decades, and has been in the Pacific Northwest his entire life. His first book, *They Were Called Records, Kids* was released in 2018 by MoonPath Press. He also created his own humorous style of haiku that he calls haikooky, and you can see his blog at: jamesrodgershaikooky.blogspot.com. James prefers his coffee with plenty of mocha.

**Marjorie Stamm Rosenfeld**, a former SMU English instructor and U.S. Navy missile analyst, has made web sites to commemorate perished European Jewish communities. Her poem "Angel" appears in *The Auschwitz Poems*. Marjorie is author of the chapbook *Fringing the Garments* (Pecan Grove Press). She says, "The powers that be have now decided that coffee is good for us. When I want coffee, I usually make the instant coffee I get from Israel and have heard that's all the rage there. I love it!"

**Don Russ** is author of *Dream Driving* (Kennesaw State University Press, 2007) and the chapbooks *Adam's Nap* (Billy Goat Press, 2005) and *World's One Heart* (The Next Review, 2015). His poem "Girl with Gerbil" was chosen for inclusion in *The Best American Poetry 2012* after it appeared in *The Cincinnati Review*.

**Rikki Santer**'s work has appeared in various publications including *Ms. Magazine, Poetry East, Margie, Hotel Amerika, The American Journal of Poetry, Slab, Crab Orchard Review, RHINO, Grimm, Slipstream, Midwest Review* and *The Main Street Rag*. Her fifth poetry collection, *Make Me That Happy*, was recently awarded an Ohioana Book Award nomination. She believes a humble Victor diner mug can transform coffee into sacramental wine. www.rikkisanter.com

**Care Santos** is the author of over 40 books in different genres, including novels, short story collections, young adult and children's books, and poetry. She has won numerous prizes and awards, including the Primavera Prize, the Ateneo Joven de Sevilla, the Gran Angular and Barco de Vapor prizes for young adult literature. Two of her books have been translated into English, the novel *Desire for Chocolate* (Alma Books) and the poetry collection *Dissection* (A Midsummer Night's Press).

**Lawrence Schimel** writes in both Spanish and English and has published over 100 books as author or anthologist in many different genres. He has won the Lambda Literary Award (twice), the Spectrum Award, the Independent Publisher Book Award, the Rhysling Award, and other honors. Recent poetry translations include *Nothing is Lost* by Jordi Doce (Shearsman), *Destruction of the Lover* by Luis Panini (Pleiades Press), and *Hamartia* by Carmen Boullosa (White Pine Press, 2019). He lives in Madrid, Spain.

**Heidi Seaborn** starts her day with two cappuccinos (bourbon optional). Her poetry has appeared in numerous journals and anthologies including *Nimrod, Mississippi Review, Penn Review, American Journal of Poetry* and in her chapbook *Finding My Way Home*. She's won or been shortlisted for over a dozen prizes. Her debut book of poetry is *Give a Girl Chaos (see what she can do)* (Mastodon, 2019). She's a NYU MFA candidate, Stanford graduate and on *The Adroit Journal* staff.

257

**R. T. Sedgwick** was born in Rome City, IN. He started each day of his first five years watching his grandfather make coffee on the kitchen range, then having a slice of bread sprinkled with brown sugar, doused in black coffee—called bread-laid-down. After breakfast, his grandfather read from *101 Famous Poems*. R. T now lives in Del Mar, CA and has two full-length poetry collections: *Left Unlatched* (2011) and *The Sky is Not the Limit* (2015). He still starts each day with black coffee.

**Su Shafer** is a creative writer and sometime poet that lives in the Pacific Northwest, where flannel shirts are acceptable as formal wear and strong coffee is a way of life. There, in a small Baba Yaga house perched near the entrance to The Hidden Forest, odd characters are brewing with the morning cup, and a strange new world is beginning to take shape...

**Marian Kaplun Shapiro** is the author of a professional book, *Second Childhood* (Norton, 1988), a poetry book, *Players In The Dream, Dreamers In The Play* (Plain View Press, 2007) and two chapbooks: *Your Third Wish*, (Finishing Line, 2007); and *The End Of The World, Announced On Wednesday* (Pudding House, 2007). Coffee mug in hand, she practices as a psychologist in Lexington, and is a five-time Senior Poet Laureate of Massachusetts. She was nominated for the Pushcart Prize in 2012.

"Anomia" was published by Poetry Society of New Hampshire, 2014.

"Waiting" appears in the *Silly Tree Anthology*, 2014

**Emily Shearer**'s poems have been published in *West Texas Literary Review*, *SWIMM*, *Clockhouse*, and *Ruminate*, among others, including the inaugural issue of *Minerva Rising*, where she now serves as Poetry Editor and Associate Book Developer. She is not supposed to have caffeine, but she does a lot of things she's not supposed to do, including swear like a trucker, drink too much, dance on tables, and blog about it at https://www.bohemilywrites.net.

Connecticut State University Distinguished Professor **Vivian Shipley** teaches at SCSU. She brews her own coffee and drinks one cup a day. Her collection *Perennial* (Negative Capability Press) was nominated for the Pulitzer Prize and named 2016 Paterson Poetry Prize Finalist. *All Your Messages Have Been Erased* (LaLit Press, 2010) won the Sheila Motton Award and the CT Press Club Prize. She won the 2017-8 Steve Kowit Poetry Prize for her poem, "Cargo." *An Archaeology of Days* is forthcoming from Negative Capability Press.

**Caroline N. Simpson** currently teaches English at Edmonds Community College, WA. She studied playwriting at Emerson College and poetry at the Ezra Pound Center for Literature, Italy. She was twice nominated for a Pushcart Prize, both in essays and poetry, and her chapbook, *Choose Your Own Adventure and other poems*, is due for publication this summer. Many of her poems have been written over coffee in one of the many unique cafes in Seattle.

"Ghost Alley Espresso" arose out of a David Wagoner exercise: no more than 4 accents per line and lines end with "r" sounds.

**Sarah Stern** is the author of *We Have Been Lucky in the Midst of Misfortune* (Kelsay Books, 2018), *But Today Is Different* (Wipf and Stock, 2014), and *Another Word for Love* (Finishing Line Press, 2011). Her poems have appeared in *Epiphany*, *New Verse News*, *Rise Up Review*, and *Verse Daily*, among others. She is a five-time winner of the Bronx Council on the Arts' BRIO Poetry Award. See more at sarahstern. me. Her favorite coffee flavor keeps changing. These days it's cinnamon pecan.

"The Interview" appears in *We Have Been Lucky in the Midst of Misfortune* (Kelsay Books, 2018).

**Diane Stone**, a former technical writer-editor, lives on Whidbey Island. Her work has been published in *Rattle, Floating Bridge Review, Adanna, Comstock Review, Main Street Rag,* and elsewhere. Her first cups of coffee—the best she's ever had—were granules of instant Sanka stirred into hot water by her grandmother. Sharing a cup of coffee was a special time to talk and reflect.

**Bruce Strand** is a Canadian poet and part-time sybarite. He likes to write about the myths and illusions we create for ourselves in order to survive life's realities. Coffee is a major player in this exploration. Notes around the laptop carry circles of dark coffee stains. If there is no coffee, wine will do. He has published poetry in some anthologies and literary journals. Bruce teaches high school.

**Jill Dalenberg Thompson** is a Chicago native, mathematician, photographer, and freelance writer. When she's not traveling the U.S. with her husband in their sixteen-foot Scamp travel trailer, she lives in Holland, Michigan, where she writes poetry and fiction full-time. She drinks coffee every day, takes it black, and will only drink from Styrofoam or paper cups in the most dire circumstances. Her poetry has appeared on *Poetry Super Highway.*

**Matthew Thorburn** is the author of six collections of poetry, including *Dear Almost* and *This Time Tomorrow.* His first book, *Subject to Change,* won the New Issues Poetry Prize. He lives in New Jersey and works in corporate communications in New York City, giving him the chance to drink coffee in two different states most mornings, and work on his poems on the bus ride in between.

"Italian Coffee" previously appeared in *Subject to Change* (New Issues Poetry & Prose, 2004).

**Meredith Trede**'s *Tenement Threnody* is from Main Street Rag Press (2016). SFA State University Press published

*Field Theory* (2011). A Toadlily Press founder, her chapbook, *Out of the Book*, appeared in *Desire Path*. Extensive journal publications include *Barrow Street, Friends Journal, Gargoyle*, and *The Paris Review*. She held Blue Mountain Center, Ragdale, Saltonstall, VCCA fellowships; the Nicholson Political Poetry Award; and a NYFA travel grant. The King's Arms (1696) was New York City's first coffeehouse. mtrede@meredithtrede.com

**Edwina Trentham**, who over the years has spent many hours in coffee shops writing poetry, taught English for twenty-seven years, edited the poetry journal, *Freshwater*, and teaches a variety of workshops throughout Connecticut. She has been a fellow at Yaddo and has been published in a number of periodicals, including *The American Scholar, Prairie Schooner*, and *Calyx*, five anthologies, and her book, *Stumbling into the Light* (Antrim House). www.edwinatrentham.com

Every morning on the banks of the San Miguel River in southwest Colorado, **Rosemerry Wahtola Trommer** grinds beans for her decaf whole milk latte. She has 11 collections of poetry, served as Colorado's third Western Slope Poet Laureate, and is poetry editor for the gourmet magazine *Edible Southwest*. She believes in the power of metaphor and teaches poetry for hospice, mindfulness retreats, women's retreats, teen programs, and more. One word mantra: *Adjust*.

**Bunkong Tuon** is the author of *Gruel* (2015) and *And So I Was Blessed* (2017), both poetry collections published by NYQ Books, and a regular contributor to *Cultural Weekly*. He is also an associate professor of English and Asian Studies at Union College, in Schenectady, NY.

**Michael Ugulini** is a freelance writer from Thorold, Ontario, Canada. His business writing includes feature articles, newsletter content, and corporate profiles. His creative writing works include poetry, short screen and play scripts, and short stories. His short screenplay *Parched* won First Place in the American Gem Short Screenplay Competition in 2006. Michael loves coffee at any time, but especially that first aromatic cup early in the morning.

Morning coffee spawned six books by **Pam Uschuk**, including *Crazy Love*, winner of an American Book Award and *Blood Flower*, her most recent. No one speaks to Pam before her morning coffee and she has written the first poem of the day. Coffee and poetry civilize her, love her, comfort her when news images clang like brass beads in motor oil. Pam is Editor-In-Chief of *Cutthroat, A Journal of the Arts* and lives in Tucson, Arizona.

**Joy Valerius** earned her bachelor's degree from the University of Arizona. Her poems have been published multiple times in *Sandscript Literary Magazine*, and she has also earned several awards for her poetry. *Dogs on the Verge of Poetry*, a collection of dog poems, is her first self-published work. Joy likes to slip a poem in between sips of coffee, both reading and writing them. She is a true "Coffee Aficionado."

A writer/poet and member of Actors' Equity, **Ron Vazzano** has performed at various NY/LA venues. His popular "Muse-Letter" is now in its fourteenth year (www.domeincapress.com), and he's been published in several literary journals including his own collection, *Shots from a Passing Car*. Following a trip to Greece 47 years ago, he never again put milk and sugar in his coffee. Drinking it black at "Grecian strength" has awakened him to the gods.

Living in Singapore, India-born **Uma Venkatraman** is a journalist with a passion for poetry. She has been published in anthologies such as *Good Morning Justice*, *Along The Shore and Beyond The Hill*, and online in *The Rising Phoenix Review*, *L'Ephemere Review*, *Amethyst Review*, and *Plath Poetry Project*.

Coffee is her favourite pick-me-up after work. She prefers making her own and likes it piping hot.

**Jack Vian**'s had numerous poems published throughout the small press world, including *Rattle*, *Poet Lore*, *Natural Bridge*, *The Kerf*, *Colere*, and *Gemini Magazine*. He won the PEN Prison Writing Award for Poetry in 2004 and *Rattle's* Neil Postman Award for Metaphor in 2016.

Under the influence of caffeine, **Catherine Wald** has written poems in *Distant, burned-out stars* (Finishing Line, 2011) and *American Journal of Nursing*, *Friends Journal*, *Gravel*, *'J' Journal*, *Jewish Literary Journal*, *Metropolitan Diary*, *Quarterday Review*, *Minerva Rising*, *Snapdragon*, and *Westchester Review*. She likes her coffee hot and her poetry scalding.

**Edward Walker**, from Guilford, Connecticut, is a member of the Guilford Poets Guild. He has an English degree from SUNY at Buffalo and enjoys writing and rewriting and rewriting poetry while drinking a bold, dark roast French press cup of coffee. When he was a child in the 1950s, his mother wrote a short story entitled "Eddie the Coffee Bean."

**Michael Waters'** books include *The Dean of Discipline* (University of Pittsburgh Press, 2018), *Celestial Joyride* (2016), *Gospel Night* (2011), and *Darling Vulgarity* (2006)— finalist for the *L.A. Times* Book Prize. A 2017 Guggenheim Fellow, recipient of five Pushcart Prizes, fellowships from the NEA, Fulbright Foundation, and NJ State Arts Council, Waters teaches at Monmouth University. He adds, "I drink only cold coffee, even in winter, brewing a pot in the evening and placing it in the refrigerator for morning. I've been negligent in not thanking coffee for its support in the acknowledgments in my books."

"Blue Collar Elegy" first appeared in *Salt Hill*.

**Steve Wilson**'s poems have appeared in journals and anthologies nationwide, as well as in three poetry collections: *Allegory Dance*, *The Singapore Express*, and *The Lost Seventh*. His latest book, *Lose to Find*, was published in 2018. He teaches at Texas State University. Over the past two summers, he has developed an addiction to the Flat White made at Alchemy in Cork, Ireland.

"Articulated Tram" was first published in *Louisiana Literature*.

**Cecilia Woloch** has published six collections of poems—most recently *Earth*, (Two Sylvias Press 2014) and *Carpathia* (BOA Editions 2009)—and a novel, *Sur la Route* (Quale Press 2014). Her honors include a fellowship from the National Endowment for the Arts and a Pushcart Prize. She leads workshops for writers around the world. Speak to her before she's had her morning Joe at your own risk.

"Flight" appeared in *Sacrifice* (Cahuenga Press, 1997).

"Waking Elsewhere" was first published in *Late* (BOA Editions, 2003).

**Sharry Phelan Wright** holds an MFA from Vermont College of Fine Arts. In 2016, her prose poem "Snapshot" was published in *Brevity* magazine. She was chosen as one of three poets to represent North Beach in the San Francisco Library's Poets Eleven contest, judged by poet laureate emeritus Jack Hirschman. Sharry lives in San Francisco's North Beach where the air is rich with the scent of roasting coffee beans.

**Stella Wulf** lives in South West France. Her work has been widely published. Publications include, *Obsessed With Pipework*, *The High Window*, *Raum*, *Prole*, *Ink Sweat & Tears*, *Rat's Ass Review*, *Sheila-Na-Gig*, and many others. Her poems have also appeared in several anthologies including, *The Very Best of 52*, *three drops*, *Clear Poetry Anthology*, and *#Me*

*Too*. She has an MA in Creative Writing, from Lancaster University. Stella is partial to a strong, dark Columbian.

"Kahveh" was first published by Prole Books, Issue 18 December 2015.

**Gary Young** is the author of a dozen books of poetry and translation, including *Even So: New and Selected Poems, No Other Life*, which won the William Carlos Williams Award, and most recently *That's What I Thought*, winner of the Lexi Rudnitsky Editor's Choice Award from Persea Press. He teaches creative writing and directs the Cowell Press at UC Santa Cruz. He'd as soon give up food as give up coffee.

"I couldn't find the mushrooms" first appeared in *Even So: New and Selected Poems* (White Pine Press, 2012).

"The rain has stopped" first appeared in *Even So: New and Selected Poems* (White Pine Press, 2012).

**Gideon Young** is a member of the Carolina African American Writers Collective. Among others, his publications include: *Backbone Press, Carve Magazine, Modern Haiku, Obsidian*, and *The Elizabeth Keckley Reader, Volume II*. Gideon is an author of *One Window's Light: A Collection of Haiku*, (Unicorn Press, 2017). He lives in Chapel Hill, NC and began drinking coffee in 2011, in Italy, backpacking on honeymoon.

"sliver of a moon" was previously published in *One Window's Light: A Collection of Haiku* (Unicorn Press, 2017).

**Jonathan Yungkans** swears his blood type must be French Roast. He is an MFA candidate at California State University, Long Beach, which has made him thankful for Peet's Coffee and Coffee Bean & Tea Leaf on campus; he has yet to try the Starbucks inside CSULB Library, but that might prove inevitable. He is author of the chapbook *Colors the Thorns Draw* (Desert Willow Press, 2018), and his work appears in *Lime Hawk*, *Twisted Vine Literary Journal*, and *West Texas Literary Review*, among others.

"Coffee" first appeared in the anthology *Snorted the Moon & Doused the Sun: An Anthology of Addiction Poetry* (For the Love of Words, 2017).

"Lift Coffee Roasters, Whittier" appears in his chapbook, *Colors the Thorns Draw* (Desert Willow Press, 2018).

**Kevin Zepper** teaches at Minnesota State University Moorhead. He is the author of four chapbooks including the forthcoming book of prose poems, *Moonman* (Playhouse Press, New Mexico). His photos regularly appear in small press magazines and webpages. His grandmother, Mary, used to "read" coffee grounds, a kind of fortune telling, for friends. Zepper sits at his kitchen table at 6 AM, drinking Maxwell House, wondering about all the wonders in the world.

## ABOUT THE EDITOR

Lorraine Healy, award-winning poet and photographer, holds an M.F.A. from New England College and a post M.F.A. in Teaching of Creative Writing from Antioch University, Los Angeles, as well as a Licenciatura in Modern Literature from her native Argentina. Called "one of the finest emerging poets" at work today by poet and critic Alicia Ostriker, Healy combines a solid grounding in the literary canon with an irrepressible playfulness with language and reverence for the natural world. In this second full-length book, Healy draws from the Spanish tradition of Machado, García Lorca, Hernández, Vallejo, and very especially, Neruda, to gaze upon her adopted Pacific Northwest landscape with luminous insight.

Healy was nominated for a Pushcart Prize in 2004 and was the first poet ever to receive American residence solely on the merits of her work. The winner of the 2009 Tebot Bach Prize, her first full-length volume *The Habit of Buenos Aires* was published in 2010, followed by the chapbook *Abraham's Voices* in 2014. Her latest collection is *Mostly Luck: Odes & Other Poems of Praise* (MoonPathPress, 2018).

Lorraine's love for vintage and simple plastic film cameras has led to an extensive writing career in the world of analog photography. She lives on Whidbey Island, Washington, where she is at work on her next poetry book.

# CONTRIBUTOR INDEX

Made in the USA
Monee, IL
06 December 2019